When I Consider
The Heavens

*The Spiritual Quest
of an Aeronautical Engineer*

Robert E. Hage

FAIR HAVENS

PUBLICATIONS

Unless otherwise indicated, Scripture quotations used in this book are from *The Holy Bible,* New International Version (NIV); copyright 1973, 1978, 1984 International Bible Society, used by permission of Zondervan Bible Publishers. Photographs of aircraft and James S. McDonnell were furnished courtesy of the Boeing Corporation and used by permission. Chuck Swindoll's story about Eddie Rickenbacker ("Old Ed") was used by permission from *Insight for Living.* The Appendix was excerpted from *This Is Old Mac Calling All the Team,* published by the author, Sanford N. McDonnell, and used by permission.

Cover design by Ed Rother, E. R. Graphics, Colorado Springs, CO
Manuscript format by Michelle VanGeest, Grand Rapids, MI

ISBN 0-9664803-6-8

Library of Congress Control Number 2003108041

Printed in the United States of America

Fair Havens Publications®
P. O. Box 1238
Gainesville, TX 76241-1238
Web Site: www.fairhavenspub.com

To my wife, Ginna,
and our four daughters:
Beth, Pam, Dana and Chris

Table of Contents

Acknowledgements 7

Foreword by Sanford N. McDonnell 9

Author's Preface 13

Chapter 1 • Off to Mars 17

Chapter 2 • God at the Controls 23

Chapter 3 • Back at Boeing in Bellevue 31

Chapter 4 • Saved in St. Louis 45

Chapter 5 • Going Out in Joy 63

Chapter 6 • All This and Heaven Too! 73

Chapter 7 • In the Garden of the Gods 87

Epilogue 109

Appendix 113

Acknowledgements

I am indebted to several friends and members of my family for encouraging me to write this story of my life. They include Al Lunsford, Monte Unger, Byron Akers, John Bass, Jim Downing, Paul Ronka, John Sloan, Betty Skinner, Marjie Barnes, Jerry White, Lorne Sanny, Herb Lockyer and Norm Rohrer.

Early in 2001 Herb Lockyer came along by my side and, observing that I was somewhat depressed, invited me to breakfast at the Garden of the Gods Club near our homes in Colorado Springs. Since then we have been meeting regularly on Saturday mornings for breakfast at the Club—praying over our writings, our families and just about everything.

Monte Unger also helped me get started and formulate early chapters, and Marjie Barnes typed the first drafts.

December 31, 2001, was a providential turning point for my book. My daughter, Dana Steers, had invited several couples from her church in San Pedro, California, for a New Year's Eve party at her home to meet her parents, who were visiting from Colorado Springs. One of the men, John Collins, was an aeronautical engineer who had used my textbook, *Airplane Performance, Stability and Control*. During our conversation he found out about my spiritual interest related to the heavens as well as my involvement with many aerospace programs at Boeing and McDonnell

Douglas over the past 50 years.

Soon after our meeting that night, he contacted a near neighbor at Hume Lake, CA, named Norman Rohrer, who founded the Christian Writers Guild, and told him about my interest in writing an autobiography. To my complete surprise, Norman called me at my home in Colorado Springs and said he wanted to help me write my life story. In April of 2002, my wife, Ginna, and I were guests for a week in his home at Hume Lake where we worked on the book and enjoyed the wonderful hospitality and new friendship of Norm and his lovely wife Virginia.

My special thanks to my dear friend Sandy McDonnell who provided the insights about his uncle, James S. McDonnell, contained in the Appendix, and who encouraged me by writing the foreword to this book.

I also want to thank Ed Rother who worked with me on the design of the book cover.

I need to give credit to the Boeing Company for providing the beautiful photos of the aircraft and spacecraft covering 100 years of flight: 1903-2003.

Most of all I thank my devoted wife of 63 years and my four precious daughters who encouraged me along the way and to whom this book is dedicated.

Foreword

Sanford N. McDonnell
President Emeritus, McDonnell Douglas Corporation

"When I consider thy heavens, the work of thy fingers,
the moon and the stars which thou hast ordained;
what is man that thou art mindful of him...?"
— Psalm 8:3,4 (KJV)

Robert E. Hage and I have spent our careers considering the heavens in one way or another. As aeronautical engineers, we were always figuratively looking up into the heavens and dreaming about making it possible for mankind to travel ever faster around the earth, to land on the moon, and to explore outer space.

I first met Bob in 1959 when he joined the McDonnell Aircraft Corporation, which in 1967 became McDonnell Douglas and then in 1997 part of Boeing. By 1959, Bob had already had an exciting and fascinating career at Boeing during the development of the 707, B-47 and B-52 programs. It became even more exciting as the years went by as he became a very important executive in the aerospace industry. Bob was primarily involved in commercial aircraft but also in military jet fighters, military transports, missiles, and manned space, beginning with the

Mercury project, followed by the Gemini and the Apollo programs. I won't elaborate further, because you will find it much more interesting as you read about it in Bob's own words.

Bob Hage, an outstanding aerospace executive, is, more importantly, one of the finest gentlemen I have ever known. Bob is completely honest in every way, and he is a warm, loving and caring person—a man of the highest character.

While Bob has spent most of his life considering the heavens from an aerospace engineering perspective, he has also been searching the heavens for answers to spiritual questions. He wanted to know how he came to be here on earth and for what purpose. Shortly after coming to McDonnell Aircraft he found the key to those answers when he invited Jesus Christ into his life. That commitment changed his life dramatically, as you will learn by reading this fascinating book.

A few years after Bob took this important step, he began in his gentle but effective way to convince me that I should make that same commitment. It took him a few years, but having gone through the same questioning phase that I was in at the time, he knew how to help me "consider the heavens" and to appreciate the tremendous benefits of inviting Christ into my life by faith, which I did in 1967. I love and admire Bob Hage very much, and I will forever be indebted to him for his ministry to me. He has helped countless others in the same way.

Bob Hage's career covered one of the most exciting periods in aerospace history: from prop aircraft to jets to supersonic transports to unmanned satellites to astronauts on the moon to space stations and beyond. And while he participated in all of those impressive developments, he never faltered in his spiritual quest. He worked hard at everything he did, and he made a difference. This world is a better place in many ways because God put Robert E. Hage on planet earth.

Author's Preface

Gazing up at the starry heavens and wondering how they all began occupied my earliest boyhood speculations about the origin and immensity of the universe. Like Huckleberry Finn in Mark Twain's classic 1884 novel, *The Adventures of Huckleberry Finn,* I observed and questioned:

We had the sky up there, all speckled with stars, and we used to lay on our backs and look up at them and discuss about whether they was made, or only just happened.

This autobiography attempts to answer Huck and all who might still be wondering "about whether they was made, or only just happened," and what we're doing about it.

Consider the phenomenal advancements of science since Mark Twain's fictional hero looked inquiringly deep into the heavens. For thousands of years, from Creation until 1900 A.D., man's top land speed for transportation was a horse at full gallop—approximately twenty-five miles an hour. Within the space of only one century, hardware now can hurtle people through the heavens at 25,000 miles per hour. What an incredible century—the 100th anniversary of the first powered flight by the Wright Brothers at Kitty Hawk!

Of these aviation pioneers the American Institute of Aeronautics and Astronautics wrote:

In 1903, the Wright brothers sent humanity soaring into the skies. In 2003, the celebration of their legacy can once again spark the finest of invention, inspire a new generation to join this historic quest, and set a course for the next 100 years of innovation in aviation and space technology. (See Photo 1)

In 1929, two years after Charles Lindbergh conquered the Atlantic Ocean alone in "The Spirit of St. Louis." (See Photo 2.) I entered high school and began my lifelong quest to better understand our big, wide wonderful universe. I learned from my study of physics that the light we observe from our nearest star, Alpha Centauri, started on its way a little over four years ago, traveling at the speed of light—186,000 miles per second. At the speed of existing manned spacecraft, flights even to the nearest star would be impossible. We can still only dream of trips to the nearest planets in our solar system.

My involvement with the space effort has led me to a new awareness of the spectacular design not only of earth but of the heavens as well—some of them billions of light years away. Imagine! Science alone can still no more explain these mysteries than it can explain the origin and nature of man and his final destiny.

The resplendency of the universe and the vast distances among the galaxies raised questions in my mind about some of the scientific explanations of creation that I had been taught. It seemed to me that only a wise and powerful Designer could have created such order. I couldn't prove it, but I became convinced that only an omnipotent Creator—God—could have made it.

My quest led to an unexpected discovery that transformed my life. I was introduced to the One who has not only created and set on course the heavens but who has also revealed Himself through His Son and through His written Word.

My mind was satisfied when I read the opening words of the Bible: "In the beginning God created the heavens and the earth." My heart responded when I heard the invitation of His Son, Jesus Christ, through the eternal record of the Scriptures: "For God so loved the world that He gave His one and only Son, that whoever believes in Him shall not perish but have eternal life."

I am in my 87th trip around the sun in this spaceship called Earth and am deeply aware of how God has guided me through nearly half a century. If, like Huckleberry Finn, you're still wondering "if they was made or only just happened," read on.

1

Off to Mars

"The heavens declare the glory of God..."
— *Psalm 19:1*

The Heavens

The thrill of celestial investigation began for me in Canada—Port Moody, a small town near Vancouver, British Columbia, where I grew up with one older brother, Dan, two younger brothers, George and Siver (a Norwegian name), with sister Mary born right in the middle. Father was a lumberman, Mother a devoted home-maker with high goals for her children.

My favorite studies included mathematics and science. As an amateur astronomer, I was fascinated by the moon, the planets, the stars—that whole fabulous celestial display. As I gazed up at Jupiter, Venus, Mars and our own moon, I wondered longingly if we would ever be able to visit them. The *Wonder World,* our family encyclopedia published in the late 1920s, ambitiously portrayed passengers leaving in open-air spaceships on journeys of several years toward our sun's planets. I read about what scientists thought was a network of canals on the red planet Mars, read novels by Edgar Rice Burroughs about the exploits of John Carter on that planet, and became obsessed by the thought of setting foot on that mysterious place.

Clear nights provided opportunities to trace in the sky outlines of men, women and animals in groups of stars called constellations. These forms were displayed in pictures by The *Wonder World Encyclopedia.* The most apparent of these sketches of imagination was the Big Dipper whose stars also formed the outline of a bear. I could easily imagine the giant warrior in the constellation of Orion with his distinctive belt of three stars, the twins in Gemini, the beautiful woman in Andromeda, and the Seven Sisters in the Pleiades described by Job:

Can you bind the beautiful Pleiades? Can you
Loose the cords of Orion? Can you bring forth
The constellations in their seasons or lead out the bear
with its cubs? Do you know the laws of the heavens?

Can you set up God's dominion over the earth?
—Job 38:31-33

Even more fascinating was looking up at the thousands upon thousands of stars in our Milky Way galaxy. I read about millions of other galaxies that stretched out to the depths of the universe and wondered where it all came to an end.

Early Schooling

My grade school in Port Moody had six classrooms and as many teachers. Miss Gladwell, our Principal, was strict about conduct and strived for perfect attendance. I can still hear her oft-repeated phrase, "I'll be glad when you do well." If we got out of line she speedily whacked our extended hands with a leather strap. In order to graduate from the eighth grade and enter high school, we were required to pass provincial examinations in mathematics, grammar, writing, spelling, geography, science and both Canadian and English history.

During my years growing up in Port Moody, I attended Sunday school in a little church near our big home and became aware of the Lord, even though I did not understand who he was. I remember singing "Jesus loves me, this I know, for the Bible tells me so...." Other songs included "Like a little candle, burning in the night" and "The B-I-B-L-E, yes that's the book for me...."

We had no copy of the Scriptures in our library at home but God graciously put his hand on me in those early days and patiently waited for a spark of faith to ignite the life-changing power of the Gospel to change my life.

Dad's lumber business above Burrard Inlet near Vancouver thrived under his skillful administration. We lived in the biggest house in town with a grass tennis court in the front yard. I learned to play tennis while still young and took golf lessons also from my Dad. Occasionally on Saturday mornings my brother Dan and I would go with Dad to a nearby golf course, have donuts and coffee for breakfast and play nine holes.

Mother faithfully encouraged me to study after dinner until bedtime—a nightly discipline that often stretched to three hours during sixth, seventh, and eighth grades.

In 1928, Dad's logging camp caught fire in a dry season and burned to the ground. My father, a heavy drinker, became depressed by the tragic loss. In 1929 when the Great Depression hit he lost everything. We moved back to my birthplace, Seattle, Washington, where I entered high school, a shy kid socially but ahead scholastically. I finished grade school in Canada in six years at the age of 12 and passed the Provincial examinations to prepare for high school.

I was afraid of girls and never had a date in high school. My Botany teacher told me once that I was the most self-conscious student she had ever taught!

No jobs were available when I graduated from Garfield High School in Seattle in 1933 at the age of 16 so I returned to high school and entered a kind of forced graduate course in literature, German, and French. I experimented in my chemistry teacher's laboratory on my own and studied qualitative analysis. Canada's advanced academic grooming gave me an advantage.

Unfortunately my father, Sigurd Hage, by then had lost his health so all he could handle were menial county jobs. I found him drunk under a tree by Lake Washington one day and tried in vain to get him home. Later I pleaded with our family doctor to "do something about it." At sixteen, I felt utterly inadequate to help him.

Mother, Mary Adeline Evans Hage, struggled to cope with this desperate situation. She became strong as she placed her hopes in the achievements of each of us kids. We were very fortunate as she helped us to study hard and excel.

I knew Dad at his best and knew him at his worst. I have always regretted that I didn't honor him in his dying days.

2

God at the Controls

Behind a frowning providence
He hides a smiling face.
—William Cowper

College Days

To enter the University of Washington in 1934 I needed about $32 (which I didn't have and couldn't get). My older brother, Dan, had preceded me by one year and owned the textbooks I would need. That was reason enough to enter engineering college, and not some other discipline. I saw this later on as yet another case of divine provision. I had no idea then what would happen eventually but I kept up my interest in the heavens by taking an elective course in astronomy.

My years at the University of Washington were a growing experience. Reserve Officer Training Corps (ROTC) activities, running on the University track team, and joining the Phi Gamma Delta fraternity helped me to gain poise and to relate better to others. I was elected president of our fraternity, president of the engineering honorary society called Tau Beta Pi, earned my big W in sports and met a lovely young student—Virginia (Ginna) Hamilton, a new freshman pledge at the Delta Gamma sorority house. My sister, Mary, attended classes with Ginna and introduced us. Ginna's brother, Ed Hamilton, was a classmate of mine in the Fiji fraternity house. He encouraged my growing relationship with Ginna. Looking back I can see the clear hand of God at work in this important encounter of my life.

At the University of Washington my main interest focused on airplanes so I majored in aeronautical engineering. In 1936, the Douglas DC-3 had just begun passenger service with major U.S. airlines. (See Photo 3.) When I graduated in 1939, commercial air transportation was well on its way to shrinking the globe. But a world war seemed imminent so instead of expanding production of passenger airplanes, the nation turned to building fighter planes and bombers. An explosion in technology was about to occur.

James Mitchener in his book, *Space,* tells about President Franklin Roosevelt convening in 1938 a group of the best scientists in the country and asking them what the U.S. could expect in new military equipment in the next few years, "if indeed the United States were to be drawn into a world war" just beginning in Europe. No one of these scientists predicted the discoveries in war years of the atom bomb, radar, the jet engine, and rocket missiles. They all were in use well before the end of the Second World War.

As president of Tau Beta Phi chapter at the University of Washington I was awarded one of only six national scholarships available that year to any engineering college in the United States. I chose M.I.T. where I earned my Master's Degree in the year just before America entered the Second World War. At M.I.T. a man named James S. McDonnell had preceded me. This tireless Scotchman would one day enter my life in the most fulfilling adventure of my career.

With my degree in hand, I could think of only one thing—heading for Tacoma to see Ginna. I arrived at her door in my red, 1936 Ford convertible. Even as we embraced, she agreed to become my wife. Proverbs 18:22 is true:

He who finds a wife finds what is good and receives favor from the Lord.

We were married on August 31, 1940. Soon afterward I became a faculty member at the University of Washington teaching aeronautical engineering courses.

America at War

Relentless preparation for war suddenly had our nation in its grip. In addition to my teaching duties, I was helping to run the university's wind tunnel, testing models of fighter aircraft like the Lockheed X P-38 "Lightning." Imagine my surprise and consternation when I received orders from the War Department to report at Galveston, Texas, to be shipped to North Africa where I would join an anti-aircraft unit. I had become a reserve officer in the Army Coast Artillery during my senior year at the University of Washington and thus was eligible for service.

I tried in every way I knew how to shift my potential service to the Army Air Corps, for which I was much better qualified, but my plea fell on deaf ears at the War Department in Washington, D.C. Red tape was thwarting any moves. There seemed to be nothing I could do to change my status, but I kept trying.

Twenty-four hours before my departure for Galveston, Texas, I received a change in orders. A general in Washington, D.C., found out about me through a fraternity brother, Bob Lamson, who outlined for the general my education and skills as an aeronautical engineer and told him a more productive place for me would be at Wright-Patterson Field in Dayton, Ohio. The general simply moved my file from the Army Coast Artillery to the Army Air Corps. Incredible! I was both stunned and relieved. I shall always be grateful to the general and my fraternity brother. In North Africa, many of my friends from the University of Washington ROTC Coast Artillery unit were wounded, some killed. I little realized at the time the full extent of God's protection and His plan for my life.

Wright Field

Arriving at Wright Field with Ginna and our one-year-old daughter Beth, I found myself with old friends from the M.I.T. graduate school working in the Aerodynamics Branch of the Aircraft Laboratory. Wright Field was the approval center for new military aircraft designs submitted by manufacturers from all over America—what a privilege to be at the center of new research and development in the United States aeronautical war effort. As a reserve officer on duty at Wright Field in Dayton, Ohio, I witnessed there an unforeseen surge of inventions and development in aeronautics during my four years of active duty.

The I-16 new experimental jet engine from England arrived one day, marking a significant milestone in propulsion. One can read in history books about the inventor, Sir Frank Whittle, Air Commodore of the Royal Air Force. During this time I had my first vision of someday applying the jet engine technology to commercial transports.

At Wright-Patterson Field I actually met James S. McDonnell, a man who would one day become my boss. Early in his career he had designed an inexpensive monoplane built modestly like Henry Ford's Model T "Flivver." "Mr. Mac" who would establish the McDonnell Corporation and build some of the world's best fighters, planned to sell his airborne flivver far and wide, but the Great Economic Depression hit at the wrong time and his endeavor failed.

During the war I developed a close friendship with Courtland D. Perkins who worked with me in the Aircraft Laboratory. Court collaborated with me on a book we entitled *Airplane Performance, Stability and Control,* a textbook published by John Wiley in 1949 and still in use. When we finished the book I was working at Boeing in Seattle as Senior Engineer in the Preliminary Design Department, and he as a professor at Princeton University's Aeronautical Engineering Department. After some 50 years and 50,000 copies, this textbook is still in print and is used today in many university aeronautical engineering courses throughout the world. It has never been revised!

Almost to St. Louis

The "war to end all wars" eventually ended in the fall of 1945. After being relieved of duties as Chief of the Aerodynamics Branch of the Aircraft Laboratory, I arranged to fly Ginna and our daughters Beth and Pamela home to Tacoma just before Christmas. They would stay with Ginna's parents. After my discharge I drove our car home early in 1946 via St. Louis where I fortuitously stayed overnight with James S. McDonnell, founder of the McDonnell Aircraft Company, whom I'd met at Wright Field.

Mr. "Mac" founded his company in July of 1939, in modest offices beside an old airport building at Lambert Field in St. Louis. By the end of that first year of business,

Mr. Mac announced with a twinkle in his eye that "the backlog of orders was zero, sales zero and earnings zero." But he kept criss-crossing the country tirelessly, searching for subcontracts to keep his company going. During the Second World War he built many of the 10,000 empennages (tails) of the Douglas C-47. General Eisenhower once called the C-47 "one of the most important contributors to winning the war." The McDonnell Aircraft Company became firmly established when the United States Navy awarded it a contract to develop the first jet-powered, carrier-based fighter.

A month after I joined my family in 1946 our third daughter, Dana, was born. While busily looking for a place to live and a place to work, I found a teaching position at the University of Washington's aeronautical department still open. However, I accepted Boeing's offer of employment at a considerable increase in salary.

In the middle of our settling in, Mr. Mac phoned to offer me a position as head of the Aerodynamics Department at McDonnell Aircraft in St. Louis. The responsibility and salary both exceeded my Boeing offer. After many confusing deliberations, I accepted Mr. Mac's offer, packed the family car for the trip, and arranged to have Ginna and our three daughters, Beth 5, Pamela 3, and Baby Dana, follow by train.

Early in a March morning, I said goodbye to a sleepy family and set off with Nicky, our cocker spaniel, and Ginna's favorite antique chair resting in the back seat. As the beauty of Mount Rainier's snow-capped peak receded in my rearview mirror I began to think hard about all that I was leaving—family, friends, vacations on Hood Canal, the friendly environment of Boeing....

On the third day out, I throttled back my new Ford to move slower and slower. Who was I fooling? I did not really wish to move to St. Louis, but I had made a commitment to Mr. Mac! In Ogden, Utah, my stress level peaked. In sheer desperation I phoned Mr. Mac and asked him to release me from my commitment. To my great relief he graciously, with disappointment, agreed with my decision. He joked that I "must have seen an image of Joseph Smith in those Utah mountains" to arrive at this decision.

Before turning around, I phoned Boeing and asked Ed Wells, vice president of engineering, if my job was still open in the Preliminary Design Department. He assured me that it was and that he welcomed my decision to work at Boeing.

Now my spirits were so high and adrenaline was pumping so strongly that I drove nonstop back to Tacoma and surprised a somewhat perplexed and confused wife. Once again, God was in control. He knew about the wonderful opportunities that awaited me at Boeing, opportunities yet unknown to me.

3

Back at Boeing in Bellevue

If a man has a talent and cannot use it,
he has failed. If he has a talent and uses
only half of it, he has partly failed. If he has
a talent and learns somehow to use the whole of it,
he has gloriously succeeded, and won
a satisfaction few men ever know.
—Thomas Wolfe

In 1940, Thomas Wolfe wrote the novel, *You Can't Go Home Again.* By the end of our third month back in Tacoma after the war, I was ready to agree with him. Struggling to find a house for my family, to handle Boeing's exacting assignments and to make the transition from military to civilian life was confusing and somewhat overwhelming. The teaching position at the University of Washington would have been fulfilling, but I doubt that we could have lived on my salary. The same house we had sold for $8,000 before the war now cost $16,000.

The Jets Take Over

"What do you want to work with, Bob?" my department head in Preliminary Design at Boeing asked, "missiles, bombers, military transports, commercial transports...?" Boeing's opportunities seemed to be limitless. The last of the Stratocruiser commercial transports had been delivered to the airlines in 1945. Now the company carefully studied several new airplane designs—all propeller driven. My suggestion was that we explore the possibilities of installing jet engines in commercial transports.

With the help of Dick Fitzsimmons, and under the capable supervision of Maynard Pennell, we set out to explore the advantages of a jet-powered airliner. After two years of study we concluded: jet-powered transport planes would be superior in many respects to all versions of propeller-driven transports. Our findings were published in 1948 by Princeton University Press. The book was based on a series of lectures I delivered that year at Princeton. The book's title was *Jet Propulsion in Commercial Air Transportation*. It outlined the benefits and advantages of jets over propellers as follows:

1. Faster – cruise speed of 500 mph instead of 325 mph, generating more passenger miles per day.
2. Smoother – flying at 35,000 feet above turbulent weather.
3. Less vibration and noise inside the cabin.
4. Lower maintenance and better safety record.

These studies impressed Boeing so much that the company built a prototype jet transport that eventually became the 707 program. In Princeton, I had told the gathered engineers:

It is believed that the development of a prototype turbojet transport…will speed the development of turbojet power plants, airport facilities, airline procedures, and the overall efficiency of the American commercial transport system.

This statement became the closing paragraph of *Jet Propulsion in Commercial Air Transportation.*

In the discussions of power plant characteristics in the Princeton Book it was pointed out that a ducted fan (later named "turbofan") would significantly increase the propulsive efficiency of the basic turbojet engine, resulting in lower fuel consumption. Nearly ten years later, the engine companies developed the turbofan and began retrofitting the turbojet engines on commercial transports permitting over-the-ocean, long-range transportation. In addition, this feature simplified the design of thrust reversers and dramatically reduced the external noise during take-off. In retrospect, an earlier development of the turbofan would have eliminated the need for noise suppressors on turbojet engines and would have greatly improved the appeal of airline travel.

For two years I engaged all my energies in the excitement of developing the potential for jet transports and jet bombers. I could hardly wait to get to work each morning. My first mission was to participate in the development of the B-47, the first bomber with swept wings—a design that led to greater subsonic speed. (See Photo 4.) Many trips to Wright Field and Air Force headquarters in Washington, D.C., kept me away from home far too long. But my job was my passion, and so my family suffered. Many years later one of my daughters accused me of being an absentee father. I didn't realize then that God comes first, family second and one's job third. For Ginna's faithful love and care extended to me and our daughters during these times I shall be forever grateful.

My Home, the Pentagon

New winds were blowing in the summer of 1949. President Harry S. Truman, elected president by popular vote, faced Russia's buildup of nuclear weapons. The Air Force petitioned me to spend a year in the Pentagon (on leave from Boeing) to work in the Weapon Systems Evaluation Group (WSEG). With our children (Beth 8, Pam 6, Dana 3), Ginna and I rented a house in Arlington Forest near the Pentagon where I spent long hours on highly classified studies. Our first study at WSEG drafted an assessment of a bomber raid on Moscow if Russia were to strike first.

During the second half of my Washington sojourn I headed a study team looking into the potential of nuclear-powered bombers. The study concluded that this would require excessive shielding around the cockpit, mechanical complexity, potential crash hazards of a training mission over populated areas, and no requirement for unlimited range. Jet bombers could reach targets in Russia and return to staging bases. Furthermore, long-range missiles with nuclear warheads could be fired on one-way missions to a designated target. The Chief of Staff of the Air Force refused to publish our report because a lot of work was going on to develop the nuclear engine. Two years later the Air Force cancelled the program, vindicating our findings.

I treasure the memories of our year in Washington, D.C. Weekends found us absorbing its history—visiting the Capitol Building, sitting in balconies while Congress was in session, climbing the Washington and Lincoln memorials, visiting The White House, and exploring the countryside surrounding our beautiful capital. Mount Vernon became a favorite.

One weekend, *sans enfants,* Ginna and I visited our good friends, the Barstows and the Perkins, in Princeton, N.J. We drove together to New York to see Mary Martin and Enzio Pinza on Broadway in "South Pacific." On another excursion with our entire families, we spent a memorable time at the beach in Ocean City, New Jersey.

On June 25, 1950, only half a decade after history's worst global conflict had ended, North Korea invaded South Korea and drew America into another deadly and costly skirmish. The Communists permanently sliced the country in two at the 38th parallel. WSEG formally requested my extended leave from Boeing so I could evaluate our weapons arsenal on-site in Korea. However, family considerations and God's providence made this invitation easy to turn down. We drove back to Bellevue where I plunged eagerly into the work of developing jet transports instead of death-dealing military hardware. Even more exciting to us was the birth of our fourth daughter, Christine.

The Prototype Pays Off

In late 1950, I was eager to begin serious studies leading to Boeing's building of jet transports, but preparations for war came first. My vision was to build a prototype jet transport that would shrink the globe and demonstrate flight above the turbulence of lower altitudes. A prototype commercial jet transport would become a $16 million gamble for the Boeing Board of Directors. However, the company's first priority was to design and build the B-52 bomber. (See Photo 5.)

The company started looking for suppliers of an engine for the B-52. Pratt and Whitney in Hartford, Connecticut, saved the day. This company announced the advent of the J-57, a jet pod of engineering perfection (two engines in each pod) offering 20,000 pounds of thrust per pod—enough thrust in four of them (80,000 pounds) to raise to the skies a 400,000-pound airplane and send it halfway around the world to drop bombs on an enemy. It didn't take our company long to obtain a government contract to build it.

Without wasting any time, Wellwood Beall, Senior VP for Engineering and Sales, now turned his attention to building a jetliner for passengers. Almost before we knew it he was on his way to Hartford to lease the prototype J-57 engines to power our prototype jet transport.

Turning to the passenger market, Bill Allen, president of Boeing, had enough courage and foresight to present the gamble to Boeing's board for final approval of a jet prototype transport named Dash 80. Building a prototype of the 707 passenger jet and demonstrating it to airline customers, he argued, "is the only way Boeing can remain competitive against Douglas in the commercial transport business." (See Photo 6.)

Boeing accomplished the goal of building the production 707 by first building a military transport version designated as the C-135 and selling it to the Air Force. Many components in the 707 passenger jet were the same as the military version, so costs were greatly reduced. (See Photo 7.)

It was no secret that our chief competitor, Douglas Aircraft in Santa Monica and Long Beach, had entered the race with a "wind tunnel" version—of a jetliner. Douglas was Top Dog in the commercial business. Its successful programs included the DC-3, DC-4, DC-6 and DC-7. Could we topple them? My cohorts and I were determined to try.

On one of my first sales trips out, I went to Sydney, Australia, to show Qantas Airlines what Boeing could deliver. Douglas salesmen had preceded me by two weeks, but they had only a paper description of the proposed DC-8. I had a 16mm movie with sound and color, showing a real live 707 prototype Dash 80 taking off and landing, and proudly displaying its interior design and cockpit operations. Our sixteen-million-dollar gamble paid off. Boeing won the contest and Qantas purchased a fleet of 707s. Boeing and Douglas see-sawed back and forth as the airlines built their fleets: United bought the DC-8, American purchased the 707. Pan American ordered both programs, and so the world grew smaller as these new transports took to the skies, "changing the way the world flies."

Honor Above Enterprise

In the race to sell our product, I learned a valuable lesson. Both the 707 and the DC-8 airplanes were virtually equal in performance and price. The final sale usually depended on the service record of the supplier, and the integrity of top officials. When United Airlines president William Patterson placed a $175 million order for 30 DC-8s, he did so even though the 707 was offered at a slightly lower price and an earlier delivery. Donald Douglas, pleased by this sizable order, asked Patterson, "Why?" "Because," Pat shot back, "I trust you. I like the way you stand behind your airplanes."

Nothing sells planes like integrity. Eddie Rickenbacker of Eastern Airlines told Donald Douglas that he would select the DC-8 if the company could suppress its noise level, as Boeing had promised. "Eddie," Donald Douglas replied, "we can't promise it."

"I know you can't," Rickenbacker replied. "I just wanted to see if you were still honest. You've just sold $165 million dollars worth of DC-8s."

Boeing had previously guaranteed greater noise control with its design of a noise suppressor mounted to the tail of the engine pod. I know because I was the one who had visited Eddie Rickenbacker a few months earlier and made that optimistic promise of a 10-decibel noise reduction. Another valuable lesson learned: Never overstate the future performance characteristics of your product!

God Dwells in a Thankful Heart

As I began to write this book, a story fell into my hands—written by Chuck Swindoll for his daily radio program *Insight For Living*. It offers another example of God's providence and one man's thankful heart:

It happened every Friday evening without fail. When the Florida sun resembled a giant orange and dipped into the blue ocean, old Ed strolled along the beach to his favorite pier carrying a bucket of shrimp. The shrimp weren't for him or for the fish. Strangely, the shrimp were for the seagulls.

Before long a thousand white dots came screeching and

squawking their way toward Ed on the pier. They enveloped him with their presence. He stood there, tossing shrimp to the hungry birds. As he did, if you listened closely, you could hear him say, "Thank you. Thank you."

Next week you could count on Ed to return and perform this same Friday evening ritual.

To those who didn't know old Ed, this looked like a meaningless exercise of an eccentric old man. That's too bad. They would have understood if they had known him better.

Old Ed was World War II hero Eddie Rickenbacker. On one of his flying missions, he and his seven-member crew went down in the ocean. Miraculously, all the men survived the crash. They floated for days on a life raft on the rough waters of the pacific. They fought the sun. They fought sharks. Most of all they fought hunger as they drifted hundreds of miles from land.

One afternoon they had a simple devotional exercise and prayed for a miracle. Then they tried to nap. Eddie pulled his military cap over his nose. Time dragged. All he could hear was the slap of the waves against the raft.

Suddenly, he felt something land on his head. A seagull! Old Ed would later describe how the bird sat perfectly still. With a flash of his hand, he grabbed it! He tore the feathers off and each man shared a morsel of it together. They used the remains for fish bait and caught more food, which gave them more bait. They were able to survive this way until they were rescued, some of them near the end of their lives.

Old Ed swore he'd never forget the sacrifice. He never stopped saying, "Thank you." So every Friday evening, he went to that same pier with a bucket full of shrimp and a heart full of gratitude to say, "Thank you. Thank you."

This true account reminds me of why we observe Easter every year. Easter is a vast "thank you" service. Easter says, "Lord God, we want You to know we'll never forget the sacrifice. You rescued us. We were at the end. Only a miracle could change things...and You came."

Meet Me In St. Louie

In the summer of 1958 I again took leave from Boeing in response to an invitation from the Air Force to participate in a think tank collective study at Woods Hole on Cape Cod just south of Boston. Ginna and three of our daughters drove with me from Seattle to New York in time to wave goodbye to our eldest daughter Beth, who had preceded us by air. With five other American Girl Scouts, Beth had been chosen to spend two months in Greece at the invitation of Queen Fredricka. Girl Scouts from other countries also participated. The Scouts visited several small towns in the poorest sections of the countryside (which had been looted by the Nazis), teaching young Greek mothers standards of nutrition and sanitation. Ginna and I were pleased for her to have this wonderful experience.

We drove on to Cape Cod where I spent two months working with the Air Force group attempting to predict future requirements for military aircraft and missiles needed for special Air Force missions. The family lived in a rented house near the beach and enjoyed a great summer vacation, swimming and learning to sail at Woods Hole.

Late summer found us all back in the station wagon

traveling toward home. We stopped in St. Louis to visit our good friends from those days during the war at Wright Field, Enid and John Aldridge—the latter now a vice president at McDonnell Aircraft. Hearing I was in town, Mr. Mac phoned to offer me a position at McDonnell to direct a program to develop a small utility jet transport for the Air Force that looked like a smaller version of the 707. I was surprised that he was still after me!

"Mr. Mac," I replied, "I have absolutely no interest in moving to St. Louis."

"In that case," he replied, "I'm coming right over to talk to you."

For the next two hours James McDonnell tried to talk me into moving to St. Louis and becoming a vice president at twice my Boeing salary. What should I do? A move would disrupt my family, force us to leave an established home with many friends, and to depart again from the beautiful Northwest.

Mr. Mac's words rang in my ears all the way to Seattle. They continued to visit my mind as I flew from Seattle to New York in the first 707 delivered to Pan American World Airways in September of 1958. Would I miss the excitement and glamor of the commercial airplane business at Boeing? I couldn't make up my mind which road to take.

A quip from famous New York Yankee's catcher Yogi Berra came to my mind: "When you come to a fork in the road, take it." This curious counsel didn't help me solve my dilemma, however.

My older brother Dan, a mechanical engineer at the

University of Washington, had helped me along the path of my career—especially in my understanding of power plant design and application. He had directed the development of the first shipboard gas turbine for the Navy and had risen rapidly to an executive position at Boeing. Unfortunately, he died a few years later from the effects of an inoperable birth defect. Dan had urged me to accept the new challenge: "Take that new position at McDonnell Aircraft Company."

Younger brother, George, having majored in electrical engineering at the University of Washington, had also moved ahead rapidly at Boeing. He became director of the lunar orbiter program at Boeing, sponsored by the Jet Propulsion Laboratory in Pasadena, California, and the National Aeronautics and Space Agency (NASA) in Houston. The unmanned space vehicle, launched to orbit the moon, sent back coveted pictures of the surface of the moon's rugged landscape. George was later loaned to NASA to become deputy director of the Apollo program. He also served as mission director for Apollos 8, 9, 10 and 11 before returning to Boeing. George's advice echoed Dan's: "Go to St. Louis."

I was still not convinced I should make the move and I didn't know then how to ask God for direction. Ginna rescued me. She was upset with our marriage, disillusioned with our "country-club" lifestyle, and just then awakening to another direction for her life. She was more than willing to move.

Matters came to a head one night, after a major

argument about our relationship. After dinner, we went walking as we often did to relieve tension. When we returned home we both became aware of a new brilliance to the myriad stars overhead in our Milky Way galaxy. We could even see clearly the Seven Sisters in the Pleiades. It seemed to us as though God were trying to tell us something, as if the heavens themselves were speaking.

I wondered what the message would be. The day of decision about the job was fast approaching. Dan had urged me to "Take the job!" George said, "Make the move!" Ginna urged me to do the same, hoping that we could find in St. Louis a more fulfilling life. Even my second daughter, Pam, at age fifteen, assured me that she would not mind changing schools at mid term. I will always remember sitting at our dining room table late one night as Pam helped me list the pros and cons of making this move to St. Louis. The pros won!

4

Saved in St. Louis

*"The final mystery is oneself. When one
has weighed the sun in the balance, and measured
the steps of the moon, and mapped out the
seven heavens star by star, there still remains oneself.
Who can calculate the orbit of his own soul?*
—Oscar Wilde, "De Profundis"

Like Solomon, I learned that "in the multitude of counselors there is safety." (Proverbs 11:14 KJV) We made our decision on Thanksgiving Day, 1958, and were all at peace about moving. We began singing "Meet me in St. Louie,

Louie," as we planned our big move to the Midwest. Mr. Mac suggested we move as soon as possible. I was to fly to St. Louis to participate in a month of orientation for my new job, fly back to Seattle for Christmas, then drive the family east for an early start on the new year—a pivotal one for every member of our family. Only Beth remained behind in Bellevue. We made arrangements for her to live with our dear friends John and Betsey Strickland until she could graduate from Bellevue High School that June. John and I were classmates at M.I.T. graduate school and worked together at Wright Field during the war.

A wonderland of snow and ice greeted us on our arrival in St. Louis on January 7, 1959. Mrs. Mac and our good friend from Wright Field days, Enid Aldridge, had set up in our new home temporary beds to sleep on that night. Our furniture would arrive in a day or two. Bright and early next day I was off to inspect my new office.

Just as I sat down to try out the chair at my new desk as Vice President in charge of the M-119 Air Force Utility Transport program, Mr. Mac phoned from New York and directed me to join him there immediately. He had set up an appointment for the following day with Juan Trippe, head of Pan American Airways, in order to brief him on a business version of the M-119 still under construction. A McDonnell secretary drove to our new house and picked up a suitcase that Ginna had quickly packed. Then I was off to New York. By the time I returned to St. Louis, the furniture had arrived for our new house so Ginna and our daughters, Pam, Dana and Chris were settled in. A feeling of "belonging" quickly gave me peace about the move.

Big Wins

1959 was a banner year for McDonnell Aircraft. The National Aeronautics and Space Administration (NASA) selected McDonnell as prime contractor for Mercury, the free world's first manned orbital spacecraft. (See Photo 9.)

On the fighter front the U.S. Navy awarded McDonnell the first contract for the carrier-based F-4 Phantom. Its performance was so outstanding that later the U.S. Marine Corps and the U.S. Air Force selected it to be their lead fighting machine. By the time production ended in 1979, more than 5,000 F-4 Phantoms had been delivered to the U.S. military and ten other nations worldwide. (See Photo 10.)

Our test flights of the M-119 were not as successful. Lockheed won the competition for the Air Force utility transport. Our version was relegated to the status of "company business jet" until its retirement a few years later. (See Photo 8.)

After the demise of the M-119 program, I became involved in planning space missions for Gemini and Apollo, as well as marketing military fighter planes and missiles. My new job title was Vice President of Sales and Service.

"Mr. Mac"

Working directly for Mr. Mac was sometimes frustrating, sometimes perplexing but always rewarding. He

demanded punctuality for all meetings in his office—
sometimes scheduled to the exact minute (e.g. 9:22
A.M.). Each of his officers could be reached directly by
inter-office "squawk" boxes sitting on our desks. We
were on constant call and hardly dared even to go to
the men's room without telling our secretaries where
we were. Lunches away from the plant were forbidden.
Mr. Mac was a diligent worker committed to excellence
and wanted his officers to imitate him.

On business trips, I was required to report to him by
telephone daily. When overseas, I would report by tele-
gram or night letter because he thought telephone con-
versations were too expensive. Thank goodness e-mail
had not been invented! He always wanted to know where
his top executives were and what they were doing. His
familiar saying to me was, "Bob, leave your trail." While
our family drove from St. Louis to Seattle to visit relatives
during one vacation, Mr. Mac once directed the state police to track me down and tell me to call the office.

Mr. Mac, though demanding, was always fair. As Vice
President of Sales, my team made many proposals to government agencies. When we won a contract, he would
call me into his office and tell me what a great job I had
done. When we lost a competition, he would tell me,
"Don't worry, Bob. There are many more competitions
down the road. You did the best you could."

Mr. Mac also knew his people, even those in the manufacturing shops that he often visited. This attention to
employees was the strength of his company.

In September of 1962, President John Kennedy and a small staff visited the McDonnell plant to review our progress on the two-man space capsule, Project Gemini. He was very interested in the space program and wanted the United States to beat the Russians to the moon. Project Apollo had not been clearly defined at that time. Before entering our plant, the President mounted a platform and spoke to some 5,000 employees gathered to welcome him. In less than 15 minutes he gave one of the most inspirational messages I have ever heard on "Why Our Nation Should Develop a Space Program To Put Men on the Moon."

After his speech he made a brief inspection of three models of the F-4 painted in the distinctive colors of the Navy, Air Force, and Marines. Then Mr. Mac escorted the President along a roped-off corridor leading to the entrance to the plant. I followed close behind, escorting Harold Brown, who later became Secretary of the Air Force. En route, the President leaned over the rope and shook hands at random with several of the 5,000 employees. Mr. Mac, calling them his teammates, told the President the name of each one and where he worked!

Surprised by God

On a summer day in 1960, a young woman named Bessie Rice came to our house to work as a cleaning lady. Little did Ginna know as she opened the door that the person standing before her would change the course of our lives for eternity. This outspoken young black woman had a smile on her face and a Bible in her hand as she set about to clean our house. Ginna wondered why she carried a Bible everywhere she went.

One time as Bessie was working she turned to Ginna and asked, "Are you saved?" Ginna looked at her blankly for a moment, unable to understand precisely what she was talking about. Ginna asked a few questions and then Bessie went back to work. Before long, Ginna asked, "What does it mean to be 'saved'?"

During the next few weeks, this young woman pressed her inquiry into the spiritual state of the Hages. She showed Ginna what the Scriptures had to say about God and the death of Jesus Christ on a cross for our sins.

I was quite suspicious about Bessie and a little perturbed because there was a lot of Bible study going on but very little cleaning. She showed Ginna the opening passage in Chapter 1 of the Gospel According to John:

In the beginning was the Word, and the Word
Was with God, and the Word was God.

She read also verse 14:

The Word became flesh and made his dwelling among us.

For the first time, Ginna understood that Jesus was God in the flesh! After Bessie had shared with Ginna many biblical insights and had prayed for my wife faithfully, Ginna opened her heart to God.

When Ginna told me she had been "born into the family of God" I understood little about what had happened; but I began to see a change in her life. She had responded to the promise in the Bible, "Believe on the Lord Jesus and you will be saved—you and your household." (Acts 16:31). Within several months from that day, three of our daughters, Pamela, Dana and Chris, trusted Christ as their Savior. Beth, our oldest daughter, was attending Wellesley College in Massachusetts during this time but made a commitment four years later to follow Christ.

As a result of Ginna's new life, she became much more adaptive to my needs and desires. Of course I thought this was absolutely great. She even baked cookies that I loved instead of serving store-bought ones. She now washed my wool socks by hand in lukewarm water so that they wouldn't shrink. I thought all this was just great, but I was skeptical about this "religious thing."

Soon after becoming a believer, Ginna attended a Bible conference at the Moody Bible Institute in Chicago. She took Bessie with her. During the meetings Ginna met a woman who also lived in St. Louis and learned about the Brentwood Bible Church near our home. Ginna and our girls soon joined that congregation. I held my ground, remaining a member in a large, liberal church.

Ginna hungered to know the Scriptures. Her desire to obey the Lord through prayer led her to a small Bible study directed by a woman associated with a group called The Navigators. Dana attended a summer Christian conference in Indiana sponsored by The Navigators and met Jack

Mayhall, director of the Great Lakes area for this organization. My daughter implored Jack to come to St. Louis and talk to her Dad because, "He's going to hell."

Jack did come and stayed in our home. We played ping-pong by the hour and even some golf on Sunday morning. His non-churchy approach impressed me. We had good talks about our accountability to God but I was not yet ready to admit my need of salvation.

I was a little like the man who slipped off the rim of the Grand Canyon and slid about 20 feet before grabbing a small shrub sticking out of the cliff. While he was yelling for help, a voice said, "I can help you, young man, but you must do exactly what I say." The man replied frantically, "Please, please—anything you say! Just let me know." Back came the voice, "Let go." As the man peered into the canyon below then up at the cliff he called back, "Is there anyone else up there who can help?"

I remained self-assured in my own ability to please a righteous God and kept hanging on. Spiritual matters were far from my mind. My work was my life. But Ginna seemed to think that God had promised her that her entire household would somehow come to be "saved." I wondered, "Saved from what?" Now and then I was forced to assess the strength of that twig and to observe the chasm below, awaiting my fall.

Immensity!

The longer I worked in the McDonnell space program the better appreciation I developed for our universe. The mind-boggling distances, the precision of orbit, the color, the curious design of the galaxies—these are enough to give any nonbeliever reason to reconsider. Science alone, I realized, could no more explain the mysteries of the galaxies far beyond our sun than it could explain the origin and nature of man and his final destiny.

In our Milky Way Galaxy, we are positioned about one-third of the way out from the center of some 50 to 100 billion other suns. The nearest sun or star to our own sun is Alpha Centauri, as mentioned in the front of this book. This is estimated to be a little over four light years away. This means that light coming from that sun takes four years to reach our earth, even though it's traveling at a speed of 186,000 miles per second.

Another way to illustrate the distance to this Alpha Centauri is to imagine ourselves in a space ship traveling at the speed at which Apollo sped to the moon (roughly 25,000 miles per hour). It would take us 100,000 years to reach our nearest star neighbor that is four light-years away. Astronomers can see other galaxies farther and farther away—some 50 billion of them that we know of today, each containing 50 to 100 billion stars of their own. The farthest group of stars is an estimated 15 billion light years away! That means it has taken 15 billion years for light to travel from there to here. Cosmologists probe deeper and deeper, but they hold little hope of reaching a rational understanding of the vastness that lies beyond our tiny home.

Ginna had obtained science articles from the Moody

Bible Institute describing the nature of both the macroscopic world and the microscopic world. In them I read that the center of the oxygen atom and surrounding electrons are directly proportional in size and distance away from the center as each one of our planets are to our own sun. Cut the atom into smaller and smaller bits and you find the same beautiful, orderly structure repeated—but without an absolute end!

The more I examined the exquisite order of the universe and the infinitesimal nature of the atom, the more I had to accept the certitude of a Creator of what we see and cannot see in the great beyond. As a scientist and an engineer, I concluded simply by faith that God is the Creator of the universe. I became absolutely convinced that only a Creator of limitless intelligence and power could have designed it.

Man, the Crowning Glory

Another mystery is the physical nature of man himself. "Is man a genetic accident wandering on a piece of matter formed by chance?" I asked myself. "Or does God have a hand in our creation?" Ginna had helped me answer this question by giving me articles published by the Moody Bible Institute, including a series of films on creation and science. By these she succeeded in influencing my thinking and caused me to question Darwinian evolution.

We know that the electronic computer was conceived and programmed by man's own computer—the brain;

"But who conceived and programmed man's brain?" I asked myself. The answer came while reading an article about the human brain in *Moody Monthly Magazine*. I learned that the brain is a wonder of micro-miniaturization that has more memory than almost any computer and more nerve lines than all the telephone lines in the world combined. The brain's equivalent of a computer's central processing unit receives electrical signals from hundreds of thousands of bio-thermometer and pressure-sensing cells, plus information from the eyes, ears and nose, and then sorts, stores and responds appropriately to them.

By the time I finished the article, I could hear the answer to my question loud and clear. Something as complex as the human brain could never have originated by mere chance any more than an airplane could somehow throw itself together. It must have a designer. I knew how to design airplanes, but only the mind of God could design the human mind and brain. I readily accepted God as the creator of my physical body.

Next I investigated the most important condition that influences the very heart of the universe—the inner man, or the soul. Man is self-centered rather than God-centered, so he continues to act without God's direction. The result is usually fear of the future, guilt, and little understanding of God's standards for him and his life.

The Bible is clear that because of man's original rebellion he became separated from the God who loves him, who created him for a purpose and who made this vast and orderly universe as a place for him to live and enjoy.

How can man possibly understand God's purpose and man's place in the world when he is out of touch with the Creator of heaven and earth and everything in it? I asked myself this question.

Heaven Came Down

In October 1961 I was traveling in Europe on business and took the opportunity to drive up to a Swiss Chalet near Villars where I spent a day with Dr. Francis Schaeffer at L'Abri (the shelter). Ginna had become acquainted with Dr. Schaeffer and his work by hearing him speak at Covenant College on one of his visits to St. Louis. She had urged me to look him up in Switzerland during a visit I made to see my daughter Pam, who was studying at the University of Lausanne.

This retreat center began in Switzerland in 1955 when Francis and Edith Schaeffer transformed their home into a safe, nurturing environment where Christians and non-Christians could seek answers to questions about God and truth. There are now L'Abri communities in countries around the world including also Holland, England, Sweden, Korea and the USA.

Dr. Schaeffer invited me to walk with him that afternoon through the breathtaking beauty of the Alps and discuss spiritual issues that each person must face. A full moon rose over the snowy peaks that evening, adding the splendor of creation to our discussions and our accountability to the Creator.

I asked all the questions I could think of concerning

the Trinity, the origin of the universe, what happens to people who have never heard about Christ's redeeming work on the cross, *etc.* Dr. Schaeffer explained each postulation simply and intelligently.

Then he turned to me and asked, "Bob, do you believe there is a God?"

I had no problem with that one. Then my host asked, "Do you feel that you have fallen short of God's standards, that you are a sinner?"

That issue had been a problem. I had lived in a permissive society where values were relative. Compared to some of my old friends, I thought I was pretty good. Compared to my new friends that visited our home from the Brentwood Bible Church and the Navigators I began to see a difference.

I knew I had fallen far short of God's standards. I had broken all of God's commandments if not in deed yet in thought. I was very sorry I had caused Ginna much pain for some of my actions. But now I knew she had forgiven me.

It seemed as though the Spirit within me was finally convicting me of the deception in my life. I know now it was also God's Spirit at work. So I admitted to Dr. Schaeffer, "Yes, I am a sinner."

Then he asked, "Do you believe that Jesus Christ was sent by God to this earth nearly two thousand years ago to die on a cross for the sins of the world; that He rose again from the dead, ascended into Heaven, and some day is coming back?"

Well, of course, I had recited the Apostle's Creed many times so I hesitatingly answered, "Yes, I believe that."

Then Dr. Schaeffer asked the determining question: "Bob, would you like to accept Jesus Christ into your heart as your own personal Savior?" I was absolutely tongue-tied! After we prayed, with no response from me, Dr. Schaeffer gently said, "Let's sleep on it." I left the next morning feeling empty, as though I had missed an opportunity.

Back in St. Louis I began to attend Brentwood Bible Church with my family. There the clear Gospel of Jesus Christ was preached every Sunday. Pastor George Johnson encouraged me to read the Bible for myself, so I plunged into a reading of the Gospel According to John for the first time. Before long, I saw a parallel developing between the faith that I had in accepting God as the Creator of the universe and faith in the Son of God as my personal Savior.

In John's Gospel, chapter 20, Thomas didn't believe that the Lord had risen because he hadn't been there when Jesus first appeared to the disciples. But eight days later, Jesus appeared again. Thomas looked at Him, saw and felt the nail print in His hand, and observed the wound in His side. "My Lord," he exclaimed, "and my God!"

Then Jesus replied, "Because you have seen Me, you have believed. Blessed are they who have not seen and yet have believed.... But these are written [in the Bible] that you might believe that Jesus is the Christ, the Son of God, and that believing you [Bob Hage] might have life through His name."

I then believed and became a child of God by faith. As I began to study the Bible it seemed to speak to me and give me purpose for my life. I could see that Christ is both the Creator and the stabilizing center of the orderly and immense universe and everything in it, yet He was not removed from my personal needs but could give me daily understanding and direction. The Apostle Paul said it well, writing in Colossians 1:17, "He is before all things, and in Him all things hold together."

I read also that "If we confess our sins, He is faithful and just to forgive us our sins and to cleanse us from all unrighteousness" (I John 1:9 KJV). What a blessing it is to know God's forgiveness when we disobey Him and yet grow in His grace, experiencing new freedom, new joy, new understanding.

At New Crossroads

Business soared at McDonnell in St. Louis. Our company became well placed with expanding military and space contracts but remained solely dependent upon the government for its livelihood. Mr. Mac wanted to continue to grow his company with contracts from the U.S. Air Force, Navy, Marine Corps and National Aeronautics and Space Agency (NASA), while at the same time acquiring an equal amount of business from the commercial sector of the economy—all within the framework of aircraft, missiles, spacecraft and associated electronics. (See Photo 11.) This balance would stabilize the ebb and flow of our company's business from year to year.

As Vice President for Advanced Product Planning at that time, I at first recommended to Mr. Mac that we acquire companies like Beech and Cessna which produced private propeller and business jet aircraft. But it soon became apparent that this type of acquisition would not fulfill the goal of equal government and commercial business. We needed to think bigger! Because I had experience at Boeing in the development of the 707 commercial jet transport, we designed and tried to market a 100-passenger twin-engine transport much like the Douglas DC-9, which came later. Unfortunately, our company lacked any commercial experience in producing such an aircraft so our attempt to sell it to American Airlines and Lufthansa failed.

Suddenly in 1966 a fortuitous opportunity presented itself. The Douglas Aircraft Company fell into serious financial difficulty—not for lack of business, but because it choked on too many orders for DC-9s and DC-8s. The costs for gearing up to meet the demand for jet transports were enormous. Training thousands of new employees caused production delays. On top of that, the Vietnam War caused shortages of labor and material from subcontractors. As 1966 drew to a close, Douglas was running out of cash. Its bankers pressured the company to merge.

Mr. Mac had seen this coming so he positioned his company to win in competition with other possible merger prospects by offering sixty-five million dollars to meet immediate payroll costs at Douglas. In the spring of 1967, I became involved by showing Douglas and the Department of Justice the complementary mix of products that would result from this merger. McDonnell had spacecraft; Douglas had rocket boosters. McDonnell had F-4 long-range fighters; Douglas had A-4 short-range attack fighters. Missile products from the two companies were also complementary and not in competition. Douglas was pre-eminent in the commercial transport business and McDonnell had none. Thus in April of 1967, McDonnell Douglas Corporation (MDC) was officially born. Mr. Mac had achieved the commercial balance for his new company!

My career stood again at a crossroads. Should I remain in St. Louis at the corporate center of MDC or should I venture out into the unknown environment at the Douglas Aircraft Company in Long Beach, California? Mr. Mac assured me of great opportunities at either location, but would not even suggest what course I should take. Would God show me the way? I turned to the Bible for direction. I read Proverbs 3:6 and was comforted: "In all your ways acknowledge Him and He will direct your paths."

5

Going Out in Joy

*"You will go out in joy and be
led forth in peace; the mountains and hills
will burst into song before you and all the trees
of the field will clap their hands."*
—Isaiah 55:12

In the early spring of 1967 I made two trips to California to ascertain my employment opportunities at the Douglas Aircraft Company in Long Beach. I'll never forget the first one. Gliding over Lake Arrowhead on its descent to LAX airport, the plane broke through the clouds

Photo 1

Arch Hoxey in Flight

Arch Hoxey, a demonstration pilot for the Wright brothers, lands his Wright Flyer at Kinloch Field near St. Louis in October 1910. Hoxey had just become the first person to fly nonstop from Springfield, Ill. To St. Louis, Mo.

(Photo courtesy Missouri Historical Society and McDonnell Douglas Corp.)

Hazey dives for the benefit of the photograph

Photo 2

Charles Lindbergh with the Spirit of St. Louis

Charles Lindbergh stands by his "Spirit of St. Louis" at Lambert Field in St. Louis in February, 1928, after flying into history on May 20, 1927, as the first person to fly nonstop across the Atlantic Ocean to Paris.

(Photo courtesy Missouri Historical Society and McDonnell Douglas Corporation)

Photo 3

DC – 3

One of the most dependable, most utilized, and most loved airplanes ever built, the legendary DC-3 was first planned as a luxury sleeper transport. This design evolved into the DC-3, which made its maiden flight from Clover Field, Santa Monica, California, in December 1935.

By 1938, the DC-3 was standard equipment on major U.S. Airlines and operating in dozens of foreign countries.

During World War II, it was the workhorse aircraft of the allied armed services. Labeled DC-3, C-47, R4D, or called "Gooney Bird," "Skytrain," "Dakota," it was "one of the five pieces of equipment that did the most to win the war," according to General Dwight D. Eisenhower.

Before production ceased, 803 were built as commercial airliners and 10,123 in military versions. Even today, DC-3's are still flying in various parts of the world.

Photo 4

B-47 Stratojet

The B-47 was the country's first swept-wing multi-engine bomber. It represented a milestone in aviation history and a revolution in aircraft design. Every large jet aircraft today is a descendant of the B-47. Boeing engineers had envisioned a jet-powered plane as early as 1943. However, wind-tunnel tests of straight-wing jet aircraft indicated that the straight wing did not use the full potential of jet-engine power.

Near the end of World War II, Boeing aerodynamicist George Schairer was in Germany as a part of a fact-finding mission. At a hidden German aeronautics laboratory, Schairer saw wind-tunnel data on swept-wing jet airplanes and sent the information home. Engineers then used the recently completed Boeing High Speed Wind Tunnel to develop and design the XB-47, with its slender, 35-degree swept-back wings.

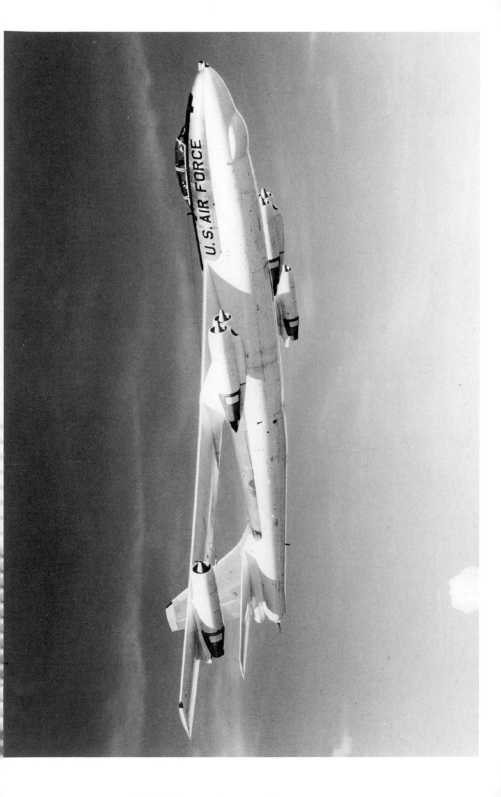

Photo 5

B-52 Stratofortress

By the 21st century, the B-52 was in its fifth decade of operational service. The eight-engine, 390,000-pound jet was the country's first long-range, swept-wing heavy bomber. It began as an intercontinental, high-altitude nuclear bomber, and its operational capabilities were adapted to meet changing defense needs.

It had a rocky beginning. The original XB-52 design, selected by the Army Air Force in 1946, was for a straight-wing, six-engine, propeller-powered heavy bomber. On Oct. 21, 1948, Boeing Chief Engineer, Ed Wells, and his design team were in Dayton, Ohio, when the Air Force's chief of bomber development told them to scrap the propellers and come up with an all-jet bomber. Over the following weekend, in a Dayton hotel room, the team designed a new eight-engine jet bomber, still called the B-52, made a scale model out of balsa wood and prepared a 33-page report.

This effort impressed the Air Force's Air Material Command, and the design was approved. As the war worsened in Korea, the Air force, in 1951, designated the B-52 the country's next intercontinental bomber and approved an initial production order for 13 B-52's. The first B-52A flew Aug. 5, 1954.

(Photo courtesy The Boeing Company, Military and Missile Systems Group, Saint Louis, Mo., all rights reserved.)

Photo 6

The Dash 80

The Boeing Company had invested $16 million (two thirds of the company's net profits from the post-war years) to build this prototype for a long-range jet aircraft. It was developed in secrecy and designated Model 367-80 to disguise it as merely an improved version of the Stratofreighter. It was subsequently nicknamed the "Dash 80," had jet engines and swept wings and was very different from the straight-wing, propeller-powered Stratofreighter. When the Dash 80 was almost finished, the company gambled again—by tooling and gearing up for a production aircraft, although neither the Air Force, nor any airline had placed a single order.

Because the prototype was constructed to sell first as a military-tanker transport, it had few windows and no seats, but had two large cargo doors. A week after its first flight, the Air Force ordered 29 tanker versions, the KC-135. The commercial version, the 707, however, faced tough competition from the Douglas DC-8. Boeing sales-people directed their efforts to Pan American World Airlines and large European airlines. On Oct. 14, Pan Am ordered 20 707s. At the same time, Pan Am ordered 25 DC-8s. The race was on.

Photo 7

Boeing 707

After the Air Force agreed to let Boeing build commercial jets based on the prototype, 367-80, already the basis for the KC-135 military tanker, airlines began to order the 707, the commercial transport variant of the Dash 80. The 707 and the KC-135 had many features in common. Both were visually distinct, with a stinger antenna pointing forward from the top of their vertical fin.

Airlines wanted the 707 fuselage to be 4 inches wider than the tanker's. Its width and the 100-foot length made it the largest passenger cabin in the air. Placement of its more than 100 windows allowed airlines to rearrange seats. Location of passenger doors on the left side, at the front and at the rear of the cabin, became standard for subsequent Boeing jets. The exteriors of the 707 and its competitor, the DC-8, were almost identical, but the 707 wing had more sweepback, so it could fly about 20 mph faster.

To get its market share, Boeing custom-designed 707 variants for different customers. Examples include making special long-range models for Qantas Airways of Australia and installing larger engines for Braniff's high-altitude South American routes. Costs of such customizing were high, so with every version of the 707, the financial risk increased. After much effort, sales of the 707 picked up. The risk-taking paid off, and the 707 outpaced the DC-8 in sales.

Photo 8

McDonnell Model 119

The McDonnell Model 119 jet transport shown during a test flight in April 1959. Model 119 was originally designed and built to Air Force requirements for a multipurpose utility and trainer airplane. It was later re-designated the Model 220 (a play on words to mark the company starting its second 20 years in business) and extensively reworked as a flight demonstrator for a proposed business jet.

(Photo courtesy The Boeing Company, Military and Missile Systems Group, Saint Louis, Mo., © 2002 all rights reserved.)

Photo 9

Mercury/Atlas 6

Launch of Mercury/Atlas 6 (MA-6) with John Glenn in Friendship 7 on America's first manned orbital space flight, February 20, 1962.

(Photo courtesy The Boeing Company, Military and Missile Systems Group, Saint Louis, Mo., © 2002 all rights reserved.)

Photo 10

McDonnell F-4 Phantom II

Three McDonnell F-4 Phantom II supersonic fighters fly in formation over the Missouri countryside in May 1963. The flight is posed to illustrate the F-4 as the "Tri-Service" fighter, having been ordered by, from the top down, the U.S. Air force, Navy and Marine Corps. All three aircraft are F-4B models.

The supersonic Phantom II is known as a multi-mission air superiority fighter, fighter/bomber, advanced interceptor, group support, tactical strike and reconnaissance aircraft. It entered combat for the first time in 1964 when the U.S. Navy used Phantom IIs as fighter escorts on the first U.S. raid against North Vietnam. Twenty-seven years later, the aircraft were used in Operation Desert Storm to destroy Iraqi radars. More recently, F-4s carried out allied military strikes on Iraq in Operation Southern Watch. The F-4 Phantom II has served the military forces of 10 other countries. McDonnell Douglas produced 5,057 Phantom IIs.

(Photo courtesy The Boeing Company, Military and Missile Systems Group, Saint Louis, Mo., © 2002 all rights reserved.)

Photo 11

Apollo/Saturn V

The July 16, 1969, launch of the giant Saturn V rocket carrying Apollo 11 and its crew to their historic landing on the moon four days later. The 363-foot-tall Saturn V was built by three of the major heritage companies that make up today's Boeing. Boeing built the rocket's massive S-1C first stage, North American Aviation built the S-II second stage, and McDonnell Douglas built the S-IVB third stage. North American also built the Apollo command and service module.

Photo 12

The DC-10

The DC-10 is a multi-range trijet transport designed to answer airline needs in the 1980's and beyond. It can carry up to 380 passengers in four commercial versions for economical operations on route segments from 300 to more than 6,000 statute miles (483 to 9,656 km).

The DC-10 is powered by advanced technology, high bypass ratio, turbofan engines, which reduce engine noise significantly, and emit no visible smoke. Features include high-lift wing devices and a fully automatic landing system for all-weather operation. It is capable of operation from relatively small airports such as New York's La Guardia with a full load bound for Chicago, or from larger airports such as Kennedy International in New York with a full load on non-stop transcontinental or intercontinental flights.

The DC-10 began operational service in August 1971. The Air Force purchased a tanker version in the late 1970s. The DC-10 fleet served 220 cities, 108 countries worldwide, and averaged more than 880 flights and 150,000 passengers daily.

Photo 13

Model 747-100/200/300/747SP

During the mid-1960s, when affordable fares caused airline passenger traffic to grow explosively, Boeing developed the first of the giant jetliners, the 747. The availability of jet engines nearly three times as powerful as those used in the 707 added to the incentive for creating the largest airplane ever built for commercial use. In addition, Boeing had a start on the design technology of such an airplane because the company had been working on, but later lost, a contract for a huge military transport, the C-5A.

Pan American World Airways placed the kickoff order for 25 747s and subsequently had an important influence on the airplane's design and on its future. The airline accelerated the development process and asked for greater range than originally intended. Boeing provided for an unprecedented cruising range of 6,000 miles and left the shorter-range versions for later. The first 747 rolled out Sept. 30, 1968, and after a year of flight tests, Pan American launched the wide-body era with a 747 flight from New York to London on Jan. 21, 1970.

Photo 14

The C-17

The C-17 logistics carrier named the "Globemaster III" combines the airlift capability of the larger C-5 with the short field performance of the C-130, allowing it to function efficiently in both forward and rear operating zones.

The C-17 is able to take off from a 7,600-foot runway carrying a 172,000-pound payload and land on an unfinished 3,000-foot airfield. Due to its advanced digital avionics system, operation of the C-17 requires only two cockpit crewmen and one loadmaster.

The first C-17 flight occurred September 21, 1991. The aircraft won the prestigious Collier Trophy in 1994 for "the greatest achievement in aeronautics or astronautics in America."

Photo 15

Hage Family Reunion
Glen Eyrie, Colorado Springs / Christmas, 2000

Photo 16

James S. McDonnell

James S. McDonnell, founder and chairman of the board, McDonnell Douglas Corporation, with the 5,000th Phantom delivered on May 24, 1978.

(Photo courtesy The Boeing Company, Military and Missile Systems Group, Saint Louis, Mo.,© 2002 all rights reserved.)

over hills covered with pine forests. The moment that sight burst into view I felt a surge of joy and peace well up inside that made me feel like singing. What would life be like in this metropolitan complex?

Approval of a merger with Douglas seemed imminent, so I assessed job opportunities in Long Beach before moving my family yet again. One position offered to me was to head a new department as Vice President for Advanced Commercial Development. My responsibility would be to develop a new wide-body commercial transport that many U.S. airlines wanted. When the president of Douglas, Jack McGowen, asked if I was after his job I feared my associates would view me as a member of an occupying army from St. Louis.

What should I do? I was torn between the security of my job in the familiar community of St. Louis over against the unknown but promising opportunities in Long Beach. Ginna suggested I take it to the Lord and ask for an answer. On the day I was to give Mr. Mac my decision, I rose early and went into the back garden of our home. I opened my Bible and asked God for direction. He led me to Isaiah Chapter 55, verses 11 through 13. Through the Scriptures, God said to me:

So is my word that goes out from my mouth: It will not return to me empty, but will accomplish what I desire and achieve the purpose for which I sent it. You will go out in joy and will be led forth in peace; the mountains and the hills will burst into song before you and all the trees of the field will clap their hands. Instead of the thorn bush will grow the <u>pine tree</u>.... This will be for the Lord's renown for an everlasting sign, which will not be destroyed.

I ran into the kitchen. "We're going!" I told Ginna, excitedly. She also was excited about this decision.

In a whirl of activities we sold our St. Louis house, drove to California, bought a house near the Douglas plant, and settled in.

My secretary at McDonnell, Marion Wheeler, was watching over me. She made most of the travel arrangements for me and the family as we moved, besides encouraging me along the way. I was reminded of my first secretary at McDonnell, Florence Vaccaro, because her expertise likewise made the transition from Seattle to St. Louis easy on the entire family. Over the years, both couples have been among our dearest friends.

I made a quick business trip to the Paris Air Show and then officially took up the mantle of my new job. I was somewhat fearful but my apprehensions vanished as we were welcomed by the Douglas executives—in particular, Jack McGowen.

Our family was scattered. Beth, our oldest, was married and lived in Boston, Pam was a senior at Connecticut College for Women in New London, and Dana a sophomore at the University of Michigan at Ann Arbor. Chris, a junior in a private high school, lived at home. The three of us began to make Long Beach home.

The Race for the Jumbos

I enthusiastically entered into work to develop the preliminary design of a new wide-body trijet, a commercial transport designated as the DC-10. (See Photo 12.) Before launching engineering and production, we needed customers and the approval of headquarters. Orders from American Airlines and United Airlines satisfied these requirements so St. Louis gave us the green light. At the same time, Lockheed began developing in Burbank, California, an almost identical trijet called the L-1011, launched with orders from Eastern and Trans World Airlines. Close competition between these two transports allowed the airlines to obtain favorable financial terms for each hotly contested sale. Consequently, neither program was a financial success. Lockheed terminated the L-1011 program after only 250 deliveries and McDonnell Douglas terminated the DC-10 two years later after 400 deliveries. An advanced model of the DC-10 named the MD-11 continued production for an additional 200 transports until the project was halted in early 2001.

Up in Seattle, Boeing had begun development of the 747 a year earlier than the DC-10 and was a more successful contender than the DC-10 and the MD-11 on the global routes of the world's airlines. The Boeing 747 is still in production after delivering more than 1,200 transports worldwide—a remarkable program! (See Photo 13.)

Wings Over the World

During my twelve years at Douglas, I worked as VP Engineering and Executive VP Marketing before retiring in 1979. Most rewarding were the last five years as head of military and commercial sales at Douglas. In addition to explaining engineering and performance requirements to each customer, negotiations for financing and good relationships with airline executives were of utmost importance.

As the top marketing executive for Douglas jets I represented the company on the delivery of the first DC-10 to many foreign carriers such as Lufthansa, Swissair, SAS, Finnair and Pakistan Airlines. Ginna and a few other executives and their wives were a part of each delivery party. We were always royally entertained by the receiving airlines at celebration parties and tours within their countries.

On one trip we flew out of New York nonstop to Karachi where Pakistani officials hosted a celebration party in our honor. We, as guests of Pakistan, flew in a small twin-engine Fokker transport to small mountain villages high in the Himalayas near K-2, the second highest mountain in the world. While landing at one small village there was no room for error. I asked the pilot what he would do if he overflew the small field and had to go around.

"I couldn't," he answered tersely, "without crashing into one of the mountains."

The airline had lost two airplanes that same year trying to approach this field in bad weather. New operating instructions demanded that pilots fly into this area only in clear weather conditions! We were privileged to stay overnight in this village's "Ritz" where water was available only in buckets. A hole in the floor served as our toilet.

Before leaving Pakistan we visited the historic Khyber Pass leading into Afghanistan. Pakistani border police were diligent in preventing illegal entry of Afghans. As trucks rolled up to the border, police would jab pitchforks into their loads of hay or big boxes to root out hidden intruders.

As we drove back to Islamabad, I thought of my first entry through this same pass en route from Kabul, Afghanistan, a few years before. It was spring, 1975. A team from Douglas flew into Kabul, seeking to sell DC-10s to Ariana Airlines of Afghanistan. After a week of negotiations, the team departed for home but I made plans to fly to Pakistan for business meetings in Islamabad. At that time, there were no direct flights from Kabul across the border to Pakistan because the two countries were at war. My only choice by air was to fly back to Tehran in Iran, thence to Karachi, and finally up to Islamabad. Unreliable flight connections would have stretched the trip to two or more days. As I studied the map I asked myself, "Why not drive?"

So I hired a driver (who didn't speak English) and a car, packed a lunch for both of us, climbed in and set off for the Khyber Pass into Pakistan some 200 miles away. Our route took us first into the Kabul Gorge and then on into the plains on the way to the pass. In 1865, 10,000

British troops had been ambushed and killed in this gorge. One medical doctor escaped to tell the tale. The following year, a British military division returned to Kabul and killed many of these ferocious tribesmen.

About halfway to Pakistan we stopped for lunch at a little turnoff and found a bench with a protective roof. Not a single automobile or any sign of civilization had appeared since we left Kabul—only an occasional group of tribesmen on horses passed, their rifles glistening in the sun. One of these groups approached our car, looked us over then rode away. God kept us out of harm's way and we reached the Khyber Pass unmolested. I imagined a headline in the Long Beach Press-Telegram reading, "Douglas Executive Disappears in Afghanistan."

The Amazing STOL

Before this chapter ends, another story must be told about a significant STOL (Short-Take-Off-and-Landing) project in which I was involved as vice president of STOL programs at Douglas. The initial interest in STOL systems began at McDonnell prior to the 1967 merger of the two companies.

In the early 1960s Marvin Marks, an associate at McDonnell, and I visited the Breguet Company in Paris to inspect a small propeller-driven STOL prototype. We were able to lease this airplane and demonstrate its short-field capabilities in several cities throughout America. STOL performance is based on the principle of powered lift. Airflow over the wing at low speeds (generated by the engine-propeller combination in this case) is deflected down against huge wing flaps lowered nearly 90 degrees from horizontal.

After the merger in 1967 Douglas started a STOL project replacing the propellers with turbofan engines for powered lift. Marvin Marks (now deceased) moved to Long Beach and was the single most important influence on the success of STOL transports for military applications.

Several study programs sponsored by the Air Force and NASA led to a competition between MDC and Boeing to build and fly prototypes. MDC won this competition, which finally led to the development of the C-17 logistics carrier. Today the C-17 transport forms the backbone of the Air Force's capability to deliver military equipment and personnel to small fields in remote areas all over the world. This growing fleet of logistic carriers was used extensively to fight the war against terrorism in Afghanistan and in the liberation of Iraq from Saddam Hussein's regime. (See Photo 14.)

At Home

On the home front, my mother had come to live with us, moving down from Seattle. Chris was still at home. Caring for mother was a lot for Ginna who was otherwise active in my traveling and entertaining.

One day our black housekeeper from St. Louis called: "Boss," she said, "the Lord has put into my heart to come to Long Beach and take care of your aging mother" (who was partially blind). So we built a new bedroom and bath above the garage, which connected directly to my mother's quarters upstairs. Bessie McCoy (not the Bessie who led Ginna to Christ) soon moved in and became good friends with my mother, watching over her and Chris as Ginna and I traveled.

Bessie is now 95 years old and lives by herself in St. Louis. She prays for each one of our extended family and we are continually in touch with her. She still calls me "Boss."

The next chapter describes how God worked through many lives to reach the heart of James S. McDonnell, the colorful Scotsman who founded McDonnell Aircraft.

6

All This and Heaven Too!

Think where man's glory
most begins and ends, and say
my glory was I had such friends.
—William Butler Yeats

We were not strangers for long in Long Beach, California. Besides enjoying the beautiful weather in this city with the largest man-made shipping harbor in the world and oceans of oil resources underneath, we enjoyed its people. At work I was warmly welcomed by the Douglas Christian Fellowship, a group of more than 500 employees who often met in the plant for lunch to enjoy Christian movies. The Fellowship also sponsored an annual banquet near the plant. In 1967, they invited me to be the guest speaker.

Ray Towne, Director of Public Relations for Douglas, met me in the elevator to our offices one day and told me he was looking for speakers for various community affairs and heard that I was "a good one." I handed him two tickets to my speaking engagement at the annual banquet of the Douglas Christian Fellowship, and invited him to bring his wife, Dorothy, to see for himself. A few weeks after my talk they joined a weekly Bible study in our home. Soon Ray made a decision to trust Christ, to the delight of Dorothy, who was already a believer.

The Lord gave me many opportunities to speak in those early years at Douglas, including Rotary Clubs, functions of The Navigators, meetings of the Christian Business Men's Committee and special church occasions. As I became bolder in my reaching out to others, I invited several of the executives with whom I worked to a Bible study early on Monday mornings in my office. We began at 7 A.M. and finished promptly at 8 A.M. Peg Foresman, my secretary, served donuts and poured coffee.

As an executive assistant, Peg was a great help to me in my new environment. She really knew the people and procedures at Douglas. In addition to her keen secretarial skills, she handled visitors and incoming communications with diplomacy and arranged my daily busy schedule of meetings and appointments. While I traveled, Peg always checked in at my home to meet any needs of Ginna, Chris and my mother.

As I traveled extensively during those early years at McDonnell Douglas I met many other people changed by God's Word and given a new dimension of leadership in their businesses. One of these was Sanford N. McDonnell who later succeeded his uncle, Mr. Mac, as Chief Executive Officer of the McDonnell Douglas Corporation.

The Balance Scale

One day in late summer of 1967 during a visit to Long Beach from St. Louis, Sandy stopped by my office after lunch. His "brief greeting" stretched to two hours, making him very late for his appointment to see Jack McGowen.

On that day, Elven Smith of The Navigators happened to be in my office—his only visit to the plant during the entire time I worked at McDonnell Douglas. After introductions, Sandy became very interested in The Navigators' work in the Los Angeles area, which Elvin directed. In St. Louis I had told Sandy about my relationship with Christ and about the work of The Navigators worldwide.

When the subject of Christianity and the Bible came up, Sandy was apprehensive about what he might have to give up by putting his trust in the Savior. "Why don't you think of a balance scale?" I suggested. "Put everything on the right side that you think you're going to give up, then we'll talk about those things that you're going to gain." We talked about his position (he aspired to move ahead in the company), about his possessions, about his pleasures, and finally about his pride (which he wanted to give up any-way). Together we read Matthew 6:33 (KJV), "Seek ye first the kingdom of God and His righteousness, and all these things shall be added unto you." I was careful to point out to Sandy that God would not add to us those possessions that dealt with the "lust of the eyes" nor those pleasures associated with the "lust of the flesh" (I John 2:16 KJV), because they were not life-giving but enslaving.

Then we looked at the other side of the balance scale and read from the Bible God's promises for a new life in Christ: that peace that passes all understanding, that new power in the life of a believer, God's gracious provision for all his needs, and finally his personal preservation for eternity. "The Lord shall preserve thy going out and thy coming in, from this time forth and even for evermore" (Psalm 121:8 KJV)—and that's everlasting life!

Two weeks later when I was in St. Louis Sandy called me into his office. "Bob," he said, "I have accepted Christ into my life as my Savior and Lord!"

"Sandy!" I replied. "What in the world brought you to this decision?"

"It was that balance scale," he explained. (See Figure 1, page 77.) "I looked at the right-hand side and I had nothing to lose except the fourth 'P', which is pride, and I already wanted to get rid of that one. Then I looked at all those 'P's on the left-hand side of the scale and I knew that I had everything to gain and nothing to lose—including eternal life. All this, and heaven too!"

Nothing to Lose and Everything to Gain —
What a Wager!
Does Your <u>Life</u> Hang in the Balance?

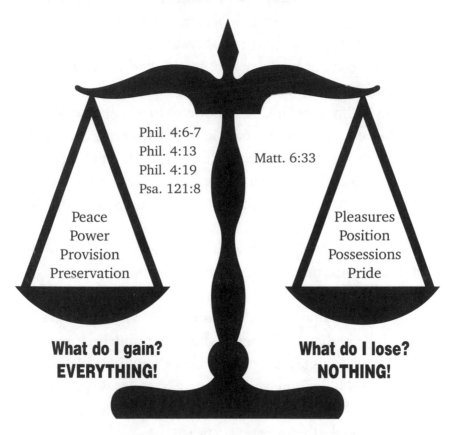

All This and Heaven Too!

FIGURE 1

Codes of Ethics

Several years later while traveling in Holland I met Fritz Philips, son of the founder of the great Philips Corporation with 400,000 employees worldwide. He showed me a printed statement of his company's philosophy of operations and a code of ethics for employees. In addition to the commitment of producing quality electronic products at competitive prices with adequate return on the investment, the statement stressed a code of integrity and ethics expected of all employees from the president on down.

The Philips code included honesty in all relationships, truthfulness in all communications, constructive cooperation in all work, fair and considerate treatment of all persons and dedication to service within the company with a view of improving the quality of life in the world in which we live.

I asked Dr. Philips, "How did you develop this code—what was your main source of information?"

"Mainly the Bible," came his reply.

We then compared the Philips code with one developed by Sandy McDonnell, which is published as the McDonnell Douglas Code of Ethics. (See Figure 2, page 79.) To Dr. Philips' amazement, the two codes were nearly identical! And since the source for each one came from the same book, this was no surprise.

Mr. Mac Meets the Master

During the twelve years between Sandy's conversion and my retirement in early 1979, Ginna and I had been in

McDonnell Douglas Code of Ethics

Integrity and ethics exist in the individual or they do not exist at all. They must be upheld by individuals or they are not upheld at all. In order for integrity and ethics to be characteristics of McDonnell Douglas, we who make up the corporation must strive to be:

- Honest and trustworthy in all our relationships.
- Reliable in carrying out assignments and responsibilities.
- Truthful and accurate in what we say and write.
- Cooperative and constructive in all work undertaken.
- Fair and considerate in our treatment of fellow employees, customers, and all other persons.
- Law abiding in all our activities.
- Committed to accomplishing all tasks in a superior way.
- Economical in utilizing company resources.
- Dedicated in service to our company and to improvement of the quality of life in the world in which we live.

Integrity and high standards of ethics require hard work, courage, and difficult choices. Consultation between employees and top management will sometimes be necessary to determine a proper course of action. Integrity and ethics may sometimes require us to forgo business opportunities. In the long run, however, we will be better served by doing what is right rather than what is expedient.

FIGURE 2

close contact with the McDonnells, visiting in our respective homes and at Navigator conferences in Colorado Springs where we now make our home. In the fall of 1979, shortly after moving from Long Beach to Colorado Springs, we drove to St. Louis to see Sandy and his wife Pris. Upon our arrival Sandy informed me that Mr. Mac wanted to see me at his home on the following Saturday morning. "What does he want?" I asked myself, since the company no longer employed me.

After a delicious breakfast with Mr. Mac, and his lovely wife nicknamed "Pussy," we two men retired to his office where I had previously spent many hours discussing company matters—Mr. Mac doing most of the talking. I knew how he was going to start the discussion before he said it: "Let's get right down to business, Bob."

But his first question took me by complete surprise: "Bob, how do you communicate with God, and how do you know He answers you?"

I had tried to talk to Mr. Mac about God many times, but had always been rebuffed. Finally I had stopped, at his request. Since I was no longer his employee, I felt complete freedom to tell him my life story, my personal testimony of how I had met Christ, how the encounter had changed my life, and how God had answered my prayers.

During our discussion we covered a wide range of spiritual concepts—the world of the occult, extra sensory perception, communicating with the dead and the power of mind over matter. I couldn't help but remember some of the names of McDonnell fighter aircraft: Banshee, Demon, Voodoo and Phantom. Before lunch we walked through the beautiful autumn foliage surrounding his home where he plied me with more questions. He asked, "Bob, if Jesus is the only way to God and all His benefits, how is it that all those Muslims in Saudi Arabia have a corner on the world's oil supply?"

I tried to explain how events leading up to the Battle of Armageddon and the return of Christ hinged on armies of the north marching to this area of the world to take over the world's oil supply. In other words, the center of action of the most important world history of all time would be the Middle East as prophesied in the Bible.

Back in Colorado Springs, I sent Mr. Mac the following letter, recapping some of our discussion:

November 1, 1979
Dear Mr. Mac:

I have been thinking back to our discussion in and about your home on October 13 and am writing to thank you for our time together and to further explore the art of communication.

When you asked me at that time how I communicated with God, I responded in some detail on why, where, when and what I prayed. When you asked how did I know I was getting through to God, I responded that He had met all my requests, changed my life, and has and is changing the lives of many others whom I know personally. I did not have the opportunity to further explain that God had been trying to get my attention for many years and it wasn't until I humbled myself and asked Jesus Christ into my life that I was able to communicate with Him through prayer and know that He was reaching me through His written Word.

Next to the Bible, the best book I have ever read on basic Christianity is enclosed. The first chapter is significant. I have met the author, John Stott, personally and have heard him preach in All Souls Church in London.

I will be in St. Louis November 8-11 and will call you. I trust we can get together again.

With warm regards,

Bob

I had no opportunity to communicate with Mr. Mac again until July of 1980. Sandy had informed me that his uncle's health was failing due to a series of minor strokes. While visiting St. Louis I was informed by Mr. Mac's secretary that he was at home recuperating. I dictated the following letter to her, which she personally delivered to his home.

18 July 1980

Dear Mr. Mac:

This morning, as I was reading the first seventeen verses of John, Chapter 3, I was led to think of you. After talking with Pussy my concerns were confirmed. I then talked to Ginna long distance in Colorado Springs

*and found that she had been praying that you would
have a fast recovery, or if the Lord decided otherwise that
you would have complete peace that you were going to
be with Him.*

*Therefore, I am moved again to urge you to read these
seventeen verses, probably not for the first time, and make
your peace with the Lord Jesus Christ. In verse 5, Jesus
told Nicodemus that we are all born physically but unless we are later born spiritually we cannot enter into
the kingdom of God.*

*As you may recall, Jesus also said in Chapter 14,
verse six, of John that "I am the way, the truth and the
life: no man cometh unto the Father but by me," and in
the Book of Revelation He also said, "I stand at the door,
and knock: if any man hear my voice, and open the door,
I will come in to him and will sup with him, and he with
me."*

*Ginna and I want you to know that we are very grate-
ful for your many kindnesses to us and our family and I
want you to know that you are the best boss I ever had.*

Our love,

Bob and Ginna

(The Bible references above are from the KJV.)

In early August, less than a month later, I received a
telephone call from Sandy saying that Mr. Mac was very
weak, partly paralyzed, couldn't talk, and was confined
to his bed at home. On all previous occasions when
Sandy had tried to speak of God to his uncle, he had been

rebuffed. Now he was troubled, not knowing how he might communicate the "good news" to his uncle before he died. I told him to go to Mr. Mac's home and talk to him about the Lord.

"What shall I say?" Sandy asked.

"Tell him your own story," I replied.

The next day Sandy was able to spend two hours with his uncle, who was sitting up, not able to talk, just listening—for a change! At the end of this visit Sandy asked Mr. Mac if he would "right now" ask Jesus Christ into his heart. He listened attentively, looking directly into Sandy's eyes. A week later Mr. Mac died at the age of 81 on August 22, 1980.

Many tributes and anecdotes of Mr. Mac's life are included in the appendix of this book, all taken from a book written and compiled by Sandy and published by him in 1999 at St. Louis. With Sandy's permission, I have included in the appendix to this book some of these stories, including Sandy's own description of his last talk with Mr. Mac.

As I look back on my life, I marvel at the way God worked in several lives to finally reach Mr. Mac—Bessie to Ginna… Ginna to me… me to Sandy… and finally Sandy to Mr. James S. McDonnell, one of the greatest pioneers of our aerospace industry.

All this, and heaven, too!

Interludes of Restoration

One summer, while I was still working at Douglas, Ginna and I took a much needed vacation and joined Elven and Joyce Smith in a rented house on the ocean at Kauai in Hawaii. Our youngest daughter Chris, still in college at the University of Colorado, went with us. I had just ended an extremely stressful period at the Douglas plant in Long Beach.

After two weeks of vigorous exercise, fighting the surf in front of our vacation house and enjoying too many dinner celebrations, we headed back to Honolulu and The Royal Hawaiian Hotel on Waikiki Beach.

The next day, Ginna and I tried surfing on the waves in front of the hotel. As we came in after our surfing lesson I looked at her and asked, "Where are we?" I didn't recognize my own daughter and our friends! Finally I turned to Ginna and said, "I know who you are."

After a hurried trip to the hotel doctor I was put to bed and fed every three hours all night long, but I don't remember any of it. The next morning my mind was clear and we flew home to Los Angeles.

A neurologist explained that the combination of stress and then vigorous exercise had contributed to my loss of memory—possibly overloading my brain's electrical circuits and causing a breakdown of the entire brain function (just like a circuit breaker in your home).

As years passed, I had a few more losses of memory for short periods of time. One incident in Vienna, Austria, caused me to think about early retirement. Ginna and I were staying at the Hilton Hotel where I hosted the President of Austrian Airlines, and his Vice President for Engineering at a business lunch. All went well until it was time to order dessert. My mind went blank and I panicked.

"Excuse me," I said, and rushed to a hotel phone to call Ginna.

"Get down here right away and help me get through this meeting," I whispered.

My wife came quickly and engaged our guests in lively conversation as I sat quietly by. It seemed as if God was telling me to slow down. Since my retirement in 1979, I have had no more losses of memory.

On another occasion in Honolulu, Ginna and I, along with her parents, were headed for Sydney, Australia, to visit Ginna's brother Ed and his family, overnighting at The Royal Hawaiian en route. As we walked up to the Clipper Club before our Pan American flight was scheduled to leave late that night, we met Billy and Ruth Graham who were flying out on the same airplane headed for Fiji and a much-needed rest after one of his crusades.

The flight was delayed so Ginna's dad spent the next hour asking Billy many questions concerning his newfound faith. I will always remember how patiently Billy gave him his undivided attention, even though he was obviously very tired. On television, Billy Graham is powerful; but on this occasion he was humble and patient with an elderly man seeking truth.

7

IN THE GARDEN OF THE GODS

"Add to these retired Leisure,
That in trim gardens takes his pleasure."
—John Milton, Il Penseroso

In the summer of 1977, Ginna and I invited Pris and Sandy McDonnell to join us at a summer conference sponsored by The Navigators in Colorado Springs. The site was beautiful Glen Eyrie, adjacent to the Garden of the Gods park, famous for its unusual rock formations.

General Palmer, who founded the city of Colorado Springs, had developed this property in the early 1900s as the site for his home. Being in the railroad business, he could import building materials such as fireplaces, exotic stones, roofing and hardwoods from all over America and Europe.

With these he constructed a magnificent 40-room castle. The 700-acre tract, castle and adjoining buildings passed through the ownership of two families before The Navigators acquired it for the headquarters of their global mission. This nondenominational Christian organization moved from Long Beach, California, to this beautiful site in 1953. At that time it had a staff of fewer than 100 workers. Today, more than 3,800 carry out the work of The Navigators worldwide.

Dawson Trotman, president and founder, died while rescuing a young girl from drowning in 1956. He was succeeded by Lorne Sanny, who is now retired after serving as president for 35 years. My good friend Jerry White is the current president.

During this Nav conference, Lorne honored the McDonnells and the Hages at a private luncheon. He seated Sandy next to him for a good visit. Just before dessert was served, Lorne turned to Sandy and said unexpectedly, and, I believe, somewhat jokingly, "When are you going to let Bob retire and move to Colorado Springs and help me run The Navigators?" To my surprise Sandy answered, "When do you want him?" Again, God's providence was at work shaping my life.

After lunch and more conversation I agreed to retire from McDonnell Douglas on my 62nd birthday anniversary 18 months in the future. Only Sandy, Mr. Mac and the president of Douglas, John Brizendine, would know of these plans until the following year. After John successfully launched the DC-10 program, he succeeded Jack McGowen as president when the latter retired. Both Jack and John had been inspirational bosses and great friends. An early agreement on my retirement date allowed my bosses plenty of time to plan for my replacement as head of marketing at Douglas without prematurely announcing my departure. Furthermore, Ginna and I found that we needed those two years to sell our Long Beach home, build a new one near Glen Eyrie, and move to Colorado Springs.

In the summer of 1978 we again spent our annual vacation at Glen Eyrie. For 15 years we had driven west from St. Louis and then east from Long Beach to enjoy a wonderful week of R & R, Bible study, and listening to inspirational speakers: Howie Hendricks, Chuck Swindoll, and Bruce Wilkinson, in addition to key Navigator staff members.

One day as Ginna and I were driving away from the conference center we passed the guarded entrance of Kissing Camels Estates, about two miles from Glen Eyrie. We wanted to purchase a house to which we could move after my retirement in March of the following year.

"Let's go into The Kissing Camels for a look around," Ginna suggested.

"We can't unless we know someone who lives there," I replied. "We can't get past the guards."

"Let's try!" Ginna said.

As the guard stopped us he said, "Oh, you've come to look at the model town home?"

Without blinking and without lying I asked, "Where is it?"

After inspecting the model home and picking out a view lot above the second green of the Kissing Camels Golf Course, we knew that God had guided us to a place that met all our requirements. The next day we purchased the home site and became the second buyers in this beautiful complex.

God was not finished directing our paths (Proverbs 3:5,6). Before we put our Long Beach home on the market, our good friend across the street, Randy Turnbow told me, "Bob, if you ever move, I want to buy your house. My wife loves it and so do I."

So, on a summer day in 1979 a few weeks after I retired, Randy and I sat on our patio overlooking the swimming pool and agreed on a purchase price—with no negotiation. The next morning we met at my bank and finalized the purchase and financing contracts. Our move-out date was open-ended and at our convenience.

Home in Colorful Colorado

In September, 1979, we moved out of our Long Beach home right on our schedule, placed our furniture in storage and drove to Colorado Springs. Beautiful autumn foliage welcomed us, and so did the staff at Glen Eyrie. Lorne Sanny invited us to stay at the Glen Eyrie Conference Center until our new home was completed. For Thanksgiving, our entire family gathered in one of the lodges for our first family reunion—all 22 of us.

Before the week ended, we were snowed in for an early winter wonderland. Our grandchildren built a snow slide from the lodge down toward the castle and adults tried some skiing. We have carried out this tradition for five more family reunions, one of which was in Austria on Wolfgang See, just south of Salzburg. Our most recent reunion accommodated 32 at Glen Eyrie, including four great grandchildren. (See Photo 15.) Our next family reunion, Lord willing, will be even bigger.

For the Lord is good; his mercy is everlasting; and his truth endureth to all generations. (Psalm 100:5 KJV)

Ministry Half a World Away

Early in 1980 we were settled into our new home on the golf course, offering a magnificent view of Pikes Peak— snow clad at this time of the year. My office was in the Navs' International Headquarters building close to Lorne Sanny and Doug Sparks, the latter in charge of the Asian ministry.

For some time The Navigators had been praying for an open door of ministry in Red China. One day Doug approached me with a bold plan. Would I be willing to visit China and survey the possibilities of placing Navigator staff in Beijing and Shanghai? I phoned my good friend Gareth Chang, then president of Douglas, China, and asked him if he could arrange a visit into China for me and Ginna. He asked me if I could lecture at Beijing University. "Fine," I replied, "but what's my subject and how do I get invited?"

"Don't worry," Gareth replied. "I'll arrange it and Douglas Aircraft will prepare a brochure and slides. We'll call it, 'The Future of the Commercial Air Transportation System in China,' based on the historical evaluation of air transports in America," which, of course, I knew well.

An invitation by the Chinese Fourth Ministry, then in charge of the Chinese airline system (CAAC) was extended to me and my wife, Ginna. Soon I was lecturing in Beijing to an audience of keen young graduate students, airline officials and members of the Fourth Ministry. Many in my audience were well acquainted with my textbook, *Airplane Performance, Stability and Control.*

Waiting at the airport in Beijing to welcome Ginna and me were a Chinese colonel and an official interpreter from the government who attended all my lectures. She later accompanied us with car and driver on a visit to the Great Wall, the Forbidden City, and many other tourist attractions.

A week later we flew to Shanghai to be met by a beautiful young Chinese woman named Tai. She had been assigned to keep track of us. Her soft, fluent English and her hospitality were a blessing. Tai escorted us to our hotel and dedicated herself to serving us, but she was not allowed by "The Party" to eat with us. However, after a few days we were permitted to have dinner with her in a small, private restaurant on the outskirts of the city. There for the first time I was able to tell her about our God who created the universe, a Savior who cares for each one of us. Tai could not grasp the concept of the Creator of the universe caring for individuals on this tiny globe. So steeped was she in Communism that she perceived God as "the opium of the people." Tai's only goal was to serve her Party diligently, hoping to be accepted some day as a full-fledged member.

At the Peace Hotel in Shanghai we met P. D. Jen, the father of a Chinese girl named Kong Mian whom we had met in Colorado Springs at a Christian conference for international students. She had written to her father, asking him to meet us when we arrived in Shanghai. While we were registering, he was hiding in the hotel lobby, waiting until Tai left. He didn't want a representative of the Communist Party to see him fraternizing with Americans.

During the Cultural Revolution, Mr. Jen and his family had been forced to leave their beautiful home and occupy a one-room flat. Furthermore, their factory, money and household artifacts had been confiscated. Later they were allowed to return to their home, occupying only one floor in their three-story house. Some of their money, along with rare artifacts, had been returned to them.

Before leaving Shanghai, we were able to visit the Jens in their home without Tai following us. P. D. gave Ginna a rare vase from the Ming Dynasty. We were warned never to reveal its owner if it were discovered in our luggage. Valuable old vases were not permitted to be taken out of China.

With Mr. Jen we attended a service in the same Protestant church that Billy Graham's wife, Ruth, attended as a girl. The sermon that morning, P. D. told us, was "uplifting" but we really didn't know what that meant. We noticed he was careful not to sign the register.

There are open doors for Christian worship in China today, and opportunities as well for Americans to be employed as teachers of the English language and as consultants in high-tech enterprises. More than 100 Navigator representatives are working in China today.

Our tickets home showed that we would fly back to Beijing, wait two days, then board a Swissair jetliner for the journey home through Athens, Greece. We were escorted to the airport in Beijing by another colonel in the Chinese military. Our luggage passed through customs without inspection, much to Ginna's relief. She had feared confiscation of her precious Ming vase. God's providence again kept us safe and allowed us to keep this beautiful gift that reminds us of the dear Jen family and their gracious hospitality. For many years we sent them a gift of the National Geographic magazine. Even today we exchange Christmas cards and pictures of each of our families. They have moved to Los Angeles and are no longer dressed in Mau jackets.

South to Another Harvest

In the Spring of 1981 we took off again, headed this time for Sao Paulo, Brazil, to be met by Dana, our third daughter, and her husband, Tom Steers—Navigator representatives. Dana had just given birth to her second child, Robert, named for both granddads. She had endured a traumatic medical episode in a Sao Paulo hospital. Shortly after Robert was born, Dana wanted to keep him in her hospital bed. The nurses refused. But after seeing no attendant for twenty-four hours, she got up, took her baby, called her husband and went home. Little Robert was suffering with a severe case of impetigo. Ginna thought it was time to go to Brazil and lend a hand.

A week after we arrived, I received a call from John Carroll, the Navigator representative in Buenos Aires. He asked me to speak at a weekend conference for couples. When Tom and I arrived at the airport in Buenos Aires, John greeted us with this news: "Bob, the conference has been cancelled but I have arranged for you to lecture to the aeronautical engineering class at the university."

"When?" I asked.

"Tomorrow," John replied. "And Bob, they are using your textbook, *Airplane Performance, Stability and Control.*

I had been away from the classroom for 40 years. What could I tell these students? Providentially, just before leaving Colorado Springs I had placed a package of slides into my briefcase, not expecting to use them on a missionary trip to South America. These were the same slides I had used in Beijing to lecture on the future of commercial air transportation. God again had anticipated all my need.

After the lecture, John announced to the students, "Mr. Hage will be lecturing tomorrow night at the public library. You are all invited to attend. His subject, however, will be somewhat different. It will be entitled, "How God Can Change Your Life."

Nine Brazilian students showed up to hear my testimony that Saturday night. Five of them appeared in John Carroll's office early on Monday morning to begin Bible study. One of those students who came to faith that fateful night, Pancho Ramirez, corresponded with me during the next few months. He invited me to return and talk to aeronautical engineering groups in two other universities. By this time he had matured in his relationship with God and his knowledge of the Bible. John Carroll's Bible classes continued to grow. Pancho and I became fast friends as we spread the Word of God. Pancho and his wife, Mayra, now live in Miami and were our houseguests in Colorado Springs during one of his leaves from his job with American Airlines.

Lessons on the Rhine

My transition from full-time employment in the aerospace industry to retirement in Colorado Springs was gradual but became almost as busy as life in full-time employ.

Ginna and I made frequent trips to visit our extended families serving as missionaries in Germany and Vienna, as well as in South America. One story took place in a hotel on the Rhine River near Bonn, Germany, in 1985. I was awakened one night by the chug... chug... chug... of the river barges carrying their cargo up river. Ginna had been listening and worrying for hours and had finally nudged me awake.

Sleepily I asked her, "What's bothering you, honey?"

"Oh, Bob," she replied, "I'm concerned for Beth."

Our eldest daughter and her husband, Paul Ronka, had recently moved to Bonn to join the work of The Navigators in Germany. Beth was suffering from depression, trying to adjust to a new language, different culture and leaving two of her four children in colleges back in America.

As we turned to the Bible and read several Psalms, we focused on verse 8 of Psalm 138:

> The Lord will perfect that which concerneth me. Thy mercy, Oh Lord, endureth forever. Forsake not the works of thine own hands. (KJV)

We both knew that God would not forsake us and that He would perfect (work out) Beth's suffering for her good and His glory. Ginna memorized Psalm 138 and recites it almost daily, knowing that God's promises in this Psalm always prevail in times of trouble.

God fulfills His purpose for each one of us. His hands not only made us but also made everything in heaven and earth and He even calls all the stars by their names. "He telleth the number of the stars; He calleth them all by their names." (Psalm 147:4 KJV)

Astronomers estimate that the number of stars in the universe is ten to the twenty-eighth power (10^{28})—a million times a million times a million times a million times ten thousand; and He calls them all by their names!

God's hands are very busy—infinite in creation yet personal in the lives of each one of us.

Great is our Lord and of great power: His understanding is infinite. Psalm 147:5 (KJV)

The Years Roll On

God has always kept His hand on me and my family and has led us by His sovereign power. He has engineered all our circumstances—most of them unknown to us at the time.

In 1983, I became a consultant to Sandy McDonnell, making quarterly visits to Long Beach to assess what was going on at the Douglas Aircraft Company. I usually stayed a week, then sent a written report to Sandy and a copy to John Brizendine, president of Douglas. John was always cooperative. As I look back today I realize that he must have felt at times that I was spying on his domain.

When Sandy retired in 1988 at the age of 65, John McDonnell, Mr. Mac's younger son, became the new CEO. At Sandy's retirement party I took the opportunity to speak about some of his leadership qualities, similar to those of King David expressed in the last two verses of Psalm 78 (courage, caring, character and competency). Some years later, one of my grandsons, David Ronka, summarized this passage on his computer. (See Figure 3, page 99.)

Three members of the MDC Board of Directors also retired that night, having reached the mandatory retirement age of 70. Since I was over 70, I knew that my

Leadership

A Lesson From David

PSALM 78:70-72
*He chose David his servant
And took him from the sheep pens;
From tending the sheep he brought Him
To be the shepherd of his people Jacob,
Of Israel his inheritance.
And David shepherded them with
Integrity of heart;
With skillful hands he led them.*

COURAGE
* David protected his sheep from marauding bears and lions with his bare hands.
* David killed the giant Goliath with a slingshot.

CARING
* God brought David "to be shepherd of his people Jacob, of Israel, his inheritance."
* David cared for his people as a shepherd cares for his sheep.

CHARACTER
* "And David shepherded them with the integrity of his heart."
* David's character flowed out of the integrity of his heart and was a key part of his leadership.

COMPETENCY
* "...with skillful hands he led them."
* David showed competence in the leadership of his people.

COURAGE   CARING   CHARACTER   COMPETENCY

FIGURE 3

consulting days were numbered and that I would soon receive a nice letter from the new CEO terminating my part-time job.

I did appreciate John's kind letter but was disappointed that I could no longer serve MDC in this fascinating industry, which had been such a fulfilling part of my life.

The B & P Ministry

A few years later my age caught up with me again. Lorne Sanny retired as Chairman of the Board of Directors of The Navigators at age 70. Sure enough, the new Chairman, Jerry White, repeated the procedure. I retired from the Board of Directors of The Navigators after 20 years of service, learning from such men as board members Howie Hendricks, Cliff Barrows, and Bob Foster, as well as from Lorne Sanny.

My service for Christ through The Navigators was not yet over. Neither was Lorne Sanny's. He felt a need to initiate a new ministry to business and professional leaders in the marketplace. He invited me and a few others to join him in formulating this new activity for The Navigators called The B & P [Business and Professional] Ministry. Wives are included because our ministry also is with couples in their homes, as well as toward men in their business environments. During my years with B & P I've had opportunities to speak to groups of men all over America: Colorado Springs, Denver, Los Angeles, St. Louis, Dallas, Des Moines, and Little Rock, as well as abroad in Brazil, Argentina, Austria, Germany, France,

Japan and China.

Leadership of B & P has passed from Lorne Sanny to Roger Fleming and now to Jim Kennedy. It's grown to a staff of 40, of which I am still a member. No thoughts of retirement, and I'll keep it that way, the Lord willing.

Home Missions

In our life at home overlooking Pike's Peak, under the red rocks of The Garden of the Gods, Ginna and I remained active. We enjoyed golf, tennis, swimming and walking— all available in our complex. Jane and Burt Dunn next door became our fast friends, so Burt and I were often on the golf course together.

After a game one morning I suggested, "Burt, how would you like to have breakfast with me next Tuesday at the club and spend some time together reading the Bible?"

"That sounds like a good idea," he replied. "Let's give it a try."

As an occasional churchgoer, my neighbor knew very little about the Scriptures, but he did have a Bible at home. I provided him with a copy of *Halley's Bible Handbook* to use as a reference.

We started reading in The Acts of the Apostles, which he thoroughly enjoyed—particularly those stories about the Apostle Paul and his harrowing adventures on missionary sojourns. Next we read The Gospel According to John but Burt had difficulty understanding parts of it, especially the concept of being "born again." At no time did I press him to take a personal step of faith.

After six months of Bible study Burt asked me one morning, "Bob, we keep reading statements from Jesus— 'It is written… it is written… it is written….' Where is it written?"

"In the Old Testament," I explained.

After pointing out to my neighbor the intent of the Old Testament and its place in the Bible, I suggested to him that we start reading in the very beginning—the Book of Genesis. Six months later we had progressed through Genesis and most of Exodus. On one Tuesday morning, Burt came to the club with a look of excitement in his eyes. We were in chapter 33 of the Book of Exodus. "What have you read for today that gives you that look?" I asked.

"It's verse thirteen," said Burt, "about Moses talking to the Lord in the tent of meetings: 'If I have found favor in your eyes [Lord], teach me your ways so I may know you and continue to find favor with you…'"

"What does that mean to you, Burt?" I asked.

He quickly replied, "Since I have accepted Jesus into my life as my Lord and Savior, I think I have found favor with God, and I want Him to teach me His ways through my study of His Word in this Bible."

Wow! What a delightful surprise it was to know that my good friend and I were now brothers in Christ.

Our Bible study group soon grew to five members, mostly recruited by Burt. We've been meeting regularly for the past 15 years at the beautiful Garden of the Gods Club near our homes. Burt died at the age of 91. The eldest member of our group, Morris Hare, went to be with the Lord five years ago. But three of us still meet: I, the teacher at 87; Sandy Mills, 87; and Ernie Turk at 89.

A few years after we men began to meet, our wives became envious of the good times their husbands were having at breakfast and Bible study on Tuesday mornings. Soon they, too, were meeting. They prevailed upon Ginna to teach them on Wednesday mornings at the Club.

During those unforgettable years of early morning fellowship around a study of the Scriptures, Sandy Mills invited Christ into his life and now speaks openly about his faith to friends and family. In August of 1999 at the rehearsal dinner for his granddaughter, Hannah, and her fiancé, Ramon, Sandy offered words of advice. I had previously sent to Sandy the following letter outlining advice and counsel for newlyweds and their life together in the years ahead. I used material drafted the previous year when I had opportunities to speak the same words of advice at the weddings of three of our grandsons. Through the years, Ginna and I have learned to practice these four reminders of commitment, acceptance, communication and forgiveness. We didn't start out that way and even today we sometimes forget, but the letter still offers appropriate reminders:

7 August 1999
Dear Sandy,

At the rehearsal dinner for Ramon and Hannah, you may want to give them these reminders concerning their life together as a married couple:

Commitment
Acceptance
Communication
Forgiveness

Marriage is a commitment to each other, under God, to love and cherish each other for life (until death do us part!).

Learn to accept one another (strengths and weaknesses) and don't try to change or criticize the other's faults. Let God do the changing.

Work on communicating clearly with each other— listen well!

Above all, remember—just as the Lord forgives us for our transgressions when we are truly sorry—learn to forgive each other.

Have fun, laugh a lot and remember to talk to the Lord every day. God bless you!

It's Always Fair Weather

When good friends get together, it's time to celebrate. To keep in touch during the busy retirement years at Colorado Springs we had arranged the first reunion of couples we knew during our sojourn in Dayton, Ohio, at Wright Field during the Second World War. We had lived in the same housing complex, played together and started our families—all in a wartime environment. We men carpooled to work at Wright Field and were involved in all phases of military aircraft development. These fortunate circumstances knitted us inseparably together.

After World War II, these couples migrated to cities all over America where the men started their careers—most of them remaining in the aircraft industry. Every two or three years we have planned some sort of reunion—first in Colorado Springs, then in Nantucket, St. Bart's in the Caribbean, the North Carolina coast, Discovery Bay in the state of Washington, Montonk in upper New York State, and most recently, on a cruise out of New Orleans on the Mississippi Belle. The passing years have diminished our group from 16 to 8, as our dear friends passed away or became incapacitated. The youngest in our group is now 83, the eldest 90 years of age. Some of our group we will see in heaven for that final and everlasting reunion.

Each year on August 31 we have celebrated the wedding anniversaries of Ginna's brother, Ed Hamilton, and his wife, Pat. We were both married on that day—we in 1940, they in 1944. Before Ed died in 2000, we had met every year for 15 years on that date—several times in Sydney, and also in Tacoma and Hawaii, and once in Montreal.

These ties that bind have drawn us close to their seven children, all residing in or near Sydney, except for one living on a 12,000-acre ranch in the Outback, 400 miles west of Sydney. Thanks to family ties, we've explored the Outback, walked on the Great Barrier Reef, and attended the Sydney Opera. Ed's funeral service took us again to Sydney, a sad occasion that brought together the entire family. Each of the seven children participated in the service. We shall see Ed again!

God Answers Prayer

On our last reunion with Ed and Pat we cruised to Alaska on the Holland-America line out of Vancouver, British Columbia. Ginna's sister Grace, and her husband Ralph, accompanied us. They lived in Tacoma and had hosted us for several of our previous reunions in their beautiful home on the grounds of the Tacoma Golf and Country Club. Sadly, just last year they both went to be with the Lord.

On our return to Vancouver, we disembarked and headed for our luggage that had been taken to a huge room near customs. Each of us grabbed a pushcart, loaded our luggage, moved through customs, and packed everything into my car. Suddenly I looked around in alarm. "Ginna," I said, "I'm missing my briefcase!"

In the commotion I vaguely remembered that I might have placed it on a separate pushcart, helped Ginna with hers and left mine behind. Back to the baggage room we hurried—no pushcart. On to customs we raced—no pushcart or briefcase there either. I became desperate.

In the middle of the huge empty room Ginna suggested, "Let's stand right here and pray that God will show us where your briefcase is." Within five minutes we spotted the brief case in a pushcart, hardly visible underneath a staircase in the customs building. Also in the pushcart was Ginna's carry-on case which, until then she hadn't realized was also missing. In it were her jewelry and other valuables!

"God," we prayed with joyful hearts, "You are so good

to us. You answer all our prayers. We praise You and thank You for what You have just done. We love You." Sometimes God answers prayers immediately; sometimes much later; but He always answers.

Citius...Altius...Fortius...

Ginna and I desire to finish strong in the years before us. In college I ran the 100-yard dash. The last 10 yards usually determined the winner of the race, provided the runner got a good start. He who finished strong, won.

At a recent Navigator conference at Glen Eyrie, Bob Foster related a story about his mother who taught him three Latin words, which are symbols of the Olympic Games—and goals for our lives:

- Citius – get going
- Altius – aim high
- Fortius – finish strong

In the 100-yard dash (or 100 meter race), the runner who gets off the starting blocks fast has an advantage. As we start each new day with a quiet time worshipping the Lord, reading the Bible, and praying, we have an advantage by getting our day off to a good start with God.

Bob Foster has written a classic little paperback book on how to plan a daily quiet time, titled: *Seven Minutes with God.* Picking up on the words his mother taught him, he elaborated on our race in life:

Citius – get with it!

Altius – we need to aim high and do our best, just as winning Olympians prepare for their races.

And finally, as we approach the end of our lives on earth,

Fortius – finish strong.

As I approach the remaining years of my life (the last 10 years or 10 yards), my goal is similar to that expressed by the Apostle Paul to the Ephesian elders in Acts 20:24: "…that I might finish my course [race] with joy…and [continue to] testify to the gospel of the grace of God." (KJV)

When his wife died in the mid-nineties, Bob Foster shared with his audience at her funeral service that for many years, he and Marion said three things before arising each morning: "Life is worth living; people are worth loving; God is worth trusting."

Ginna and I echo those words as we awaken each morning. And we plan to repeat them with a joyful heart for all of our remaining days on planet earth.

Just as Huckleberry Finn enjoyed gazing at "the sky up there, all speckled with stars," we also do to this day. Unlike Huck, we don't have to wonder "whether they was made, or only just happened" because the Bible tells us plainly in Paul's Epistle to the Romans, "The invisible things of Him from the creation of the world are clearly seen, being understood by the things that are made, even his eternal power and Godhead, so that all are without excuse."

Life is worth living; people are worth loving; and God is worth trusting.

Epilogue

My story begins with a childhood dream of some day going to the planet Mars. The story ends in this book, nearing the finish of my 87th trip around the sun.

Manned missions to Mars seem unlikely for many years to come. Our unmanned probes to the martian landscape reveal a barren and rocky surface devoid of water and life of any kind.

Without a national directive like "beat the Russians to the moon," which the Apollo program enjoyed under President Kennedy, a martian mission would seem unsupportable, considering a cost of hundreds of billions of dollars. Technically it could be accomplished by assembling a huge space station in Earth orbit and then launching a space vehicle towards Mars—equipped to support a flight of about one year to the planet Mars, carrying a separate landing vehicle, a rendezvous vehicle to explore the surface of Mars, and then returning to Earth. Life support for the crew on a two-year mission would be a problem!

Politically, such a mission would rank low in national priority, far down the list from our war against world terrorism, homeland security and economic prosperity.

Manned trips to the outer planets in our solar system are unthinkable, requiring a lifetime to reach environments unsuitable for any kind of life. Our other near neighbors, Mercury and Venus, are much too hot to attempt landing and exploring the landscapes.

Manned missions to the stars can only be fantasized—like the movie "Star Wars." Imagine this: A space vehicle traveling the speed at which Apollo cruised to the moon would take 100,000 years to reach our nearest star neighbor! Even at the speed of light, a trip across our Milky Way Galaxy would take 100,000 years. Then there are fifty billion other galaxies billions of light years away! I wonder what this all means about the possibility of life like ours somewhere in the entire universe?

Hugh Ross, in his recent book, *The Creator and the Cosmos,* describes an environment on earth so delicately balanced and fine-tuned that any small change in the age and nature of our solar system and in our Milky Way Galaxy would make life on Earth impossible. Even though there are billions of stars in the universe, some with surrounding planets, life like ours seems highly improbable.

Ross describes 66 different and narrowly defined physical and chemical conditions that must exist in our own galaxy in order for life on this planet to exist. Our galaxy must have the right age and shape to support a stable solar system with its nine planets. Jupiter and Saturn are positioned to intercept stray asteroids and comets that could obliterate the Earth. Our moon's size, orbit and distance from Earth are just right to make life on Earth possible. Earth's elliptical orbit around the sun and the length of our 24-hour day permit livable temperatures, *etc.*

Hugh Ross concludes that the estimated probability (or chance) of attaining all of the necessary parameters for life on Earth is far, far less than the number of planets in the universe where life like ours might occur—one chance in 10^{144} (a trillion multiplied by itself 12 times!) that even one such planet would exist in the entire universe.

God the Creator made you and me "in His image" and I believe as unique residents in the entire universe. The Bible states that Jesus Christ died once for all of us at a particular time and place on this earth. "God so loved the world that He gave His one and only Son...."

WHEN I CONSIDER THE HEAVENS...

Anecdote on the Heavens

Sherlock Holmes and Dr. Watson went on a camping trip. As they lay down for the night, Holmes said: "Watson, look up into the sky and tell me what you see."

Watson said, "I see millions and millions of stars."

Holmes then asked, "And what does that tell you?"

"Astronomically," Watson began, "it tells me that there are millions of galaxies and potentially billions of planets. Theologically, it tells me that God is great, and that we are small and insignificant. Meteorologically, it tells me that we will have a beautiful day tomorrow. What does it tell you?"

"Well," Holmes began, "it tells me that somebody stole our tent."

—Author unknown

Appendix

In 1999 Sanford N. McDonnell (Sandy) compiled and published a book entitled *This Is Old Mac Calling All the Team,* which is the story of James S. McDonnell and McDonnell Douglas.

Sandy went to work for his uncle James S. McDonnell in 1948, when McDonnell Aircraft Corporation was only nine years old and had about 4,500 employees. When Mr. Mac died in 1980, Sandy succeeded him as Chairman and Chief Executive Officer of the McDonnell Douglas Corporation. Sandy retired in 1988 and has dedicated himself to developing moral character and civic virtue in our nation's young people as one way of promoting a more compassionate and responsible society.

With the permission of Sandy, I have quoted in the following passages some of his intimate impressions of Mr. Mac, as well as those from teammates and associates. These vignettes and anecdotes reveal a somewhat complex and truly great man who made key contributions to the world of aerospace in the twentieth century.

James Smith McDonnell

...Was an American Aviation Pioneer who made aviation history during his eighty-one years on what he often referred to as "Planet Earth." He was born in 1899, four years before the Wright brothers made their first flight at Kitty Hawk.

He decided on a career in aviation while he was still at Princeton University, and he set a goal for himself that he would start his own aircraft company by the time he was forty years of age. He felt that he needed to be thoroughly prepared for that milestone and tried hard to get experience in every key discipline needed to be successful in the corporate world. At one point he even offered to work at zero salary if he could have a job in manufacturing at one aircraft corporation. (He didn't get the job!)

By the time he was forty he decided he was ready, and in 1939 he started the McDonnell Aircraft Corporation in St. Louis, Missouri. He had $35,000 of his own money and loans and commitments totaling another $135,000.

"Mr. Mac," as his employees called him, was intrigued by a statue by sculptor Albin Polasek of a powerful man with hammer and chisel literally carving out his own body from the stone that imprisoned him. It was called, "Man Carving Out His Destiny," and that was a succinct metaphor for Mr. Mac's life. He started life at the birth of aviation when the first aircraft could only fly very short distances. By the time of his death in 1980, he had helped make possible supersonic flight, manned space stations, and men on the moon.

Mr. Mac was a classic example of what a person living in the United States of America can accomplish in our free enterprise system—not only in his chosen career, but also in service to mankind. He worked hard to preserve world peace through the United Nations and NATO. He worked hard to promote science and education in general. He worked hard at everything he did, and he made a difference. This world is a better place in many ways because of the existence of James Smith McDonnell. (See Photo 16.)

Recollections of
SANFORD N. McDONNELL
Chairman and Chief Executive Officer, McDonnell Douglas Corporation, who retired in 1988 after 39 years of service

When I hired in at McDonnell Aircraft Corporation on 5 October 1948, there were approximately 4,500 employees. Mr. Mac asked that I drop by for breakfast that morning. At that time he suggested that I start work at the lowest wage paid, which happened to be 70 cents an hour for janitors. He explained that it would be nice for me to be able to look back in years ahead and say that I had started at the very bottom like Bill Orthwein. My reaction (which I kept to myself) was that Bill was a liberal arts graduate from Yale and didn't deserve any higher pay. I thanked Mr. Mac for his creative idea but chose to go to work at the going rate for engineering graduates at that time: $1.26 per hour.

In the early sixties, Kendall Perkins decided that the McDonnell Company needed a strategic plan. He brought in a specialist in strategic planning and gathered all of the top management except Mr. Mac, who was unaware of the meeting or its purpose. When Mr. Mac found out that all of his top people were in Ken Perkins' office, he got Ken on the phone and told him to adjourn the meeting, gather up all the papers, and come to his office. At that point, he informed Ken, "You should understand that I am the only strategic planner in this corporation."

Mr. Mac had a tremendous capacity for detail. In our meetings with him, many of us often felt that he carried it too far. More often than not, however, he would discover an important detail of the problem we were studying that none of us had thought of. When he could not come up with a good solution to a specific problem after a long session, he would adjourn the meeting and say that we should all "sleep on it." He used his subconscious mind very effectively and almost always came back the next morning with the right answer or solution.

In July 1972, when I was the corporate president of McDonnell Douglas, Mr. Mac got a call from Bob Six, the CEO of Continental Airlines. Bob chewed out Mr. Mac for half an hour because a newly delivered DC-10 had lost part of its number two engine into the backyard of a Hollywood home. No one was hurt, but there could have been a serious accident. At the end of the harangue, Six told Mr. Mac, "I want the CEO of McDonnell Douglas in my office in Los Angeles at eight Monday morning!" Mr. Mac replied, "Yes, sir." The next day, under New Business at the McDonnell Douglas Board meeting, Mr. Mac said, "Gentlemen, I think Sandy is ready to become the CEO." And I was in Los Angeles the following Monday morning getting chewed out in person by Bob Six.

A few weeks later, I found out what it meant to be the CEO when the founder was still very much around. I had a disagreement with Mr. Mac on a business matter. After a 30-minute discussion, I said, "Mr. Mac, now that I am the CEO, I will take the responsibility for doing this my way." He replied, "Sandy, there is something you don't understand. You may be the CEO, but I'm still the boss!" And he was until he died in 1980.

In preparation for the May 1975 shareholders' meeting, we heard a rumor that a large number of Vietnam protesters planned to attend and would very likely disrupt the meeting. Mr. Mac decided that this was a good opportunity for me to chair the shareholders' meeting, so I trained for it with a number of mock sessions with my associates giving me nasty questions or performing in disruptive ways. At the actual meeting, I was almost disappointed that nothing really unusual happened. Mr. Mac sat in the audience and, apparently, had not been recognized by most of the shareholders. After the meeting, however, he sent me one of the brown envelopes that had been given to each shareholder as they came into the meeting. The envelope contained a proxy statement, a questionnaire, the agenda, and a wooden pencil. On the envelope, Mr. Mac wrote in his large hand, "To SNM from JSM re Shareholders' Meeting. 1. WELL DONE. 2. Most shareholders bring their own pencils and those who don't can borrow from others. Let's save the cost of the wooden pencils next year."

All through his life, Mr. Mac was intensely interested in the spiritual side of life, and he named all of the early fighters after the spirit world: e.g., Phantom, Demon, Goblin, Banshee, Voodoo. Although he did not believe in the divinity of Jesus Christ, he did believe in a Supreme Being, as indicated by the following prayer which he often gave at family dinners when asked to say grace:

"Universal Creative Spirit—
We thank you for the gift of conscious life on Earth with the opportunity to explore, create, develop, and grow in spirit and the opportunity to nurture all living things and take charge of the creative evolution of same.
Hallelujah!"

Knowing that I was a Christian, he debated and questioned me a number of times about my faith. Then one day he said, "I won't proselytize you any more if you won't proselytize me."

Just a few weeks before his death when he was incapacitated by a series of strokes, I visited with him one-on-one for the last time. He appeared to understand everything that I said, but could not respond verbally. I took that opportunity to witness to him, which was perhaps the only time I was ever able to dominate a conversation between the two of us. I recited Revelation 3:20 and recommended to him that he accept Christ into his life—that he had nothing to lose and much to gain. Looking me squarely in the eye, he apparently took it all in. Whether he took my suggestion or not, I will never know. But for whatever it was worth, I did get the last word!

Recollections of
GEORGE S. GRAFF
President, McDonnell Aircraft Company,
who retired in 1982 after 40 years of service

The most memorable anecdote I have is associated with the chartered DC-3 airplane trip to Wright Patterson to present the case for the Model 119 as the Air Force's next personnel transport. The accident report by Buck Rogers tells the story quite succinctly, particularly when he describes the exodus from the burning aircraft. There are some details, however, that he omitted.

Just west of Connersville, Indiana, the right engine threw a cylinder and burst into flames. We made a very fortuitous emergency landing at the Connersville Airport with the right engine and nacelle burning fiercely. As we were making our way out of the burning DC-3 "in an orderly manner but in no particular order," Mr. Mac remained calmly seated and called out to us, "Gentlemen, don't forget your briefcases." I am not ashamed to say that on that occasion I paid no attention to what he said. He was the last passenger to leave, pushed along by the two pilots.

After taking over the Connersville Airport manager's office, commandeering every available telephone in the airport, he made arrangements for the Air Force to pick up the team and transport us to Wright Patterson in another DC-3. Before we began our presentation to the experts at the field, Mr. Mac asked if he might say a few words of introduction. I can't vouch that these are his exact words, but they are not far from them.

"Gentlemen," he began, "for almost 25 years the DC-3 has been the backbone of this country's commercial and military transportation systems. But today I am here to tell you from personal experience that it is time you retired that airplane!"

That brought the house down. Even the still-shaken MAC team had to laugh.

Fortunately, the Air Force didn't buy the Model 119; they chose the Lockheed Jetstar instead. I say "fortunately," because Lockheed lost a bundle on it. Sometime later, Mr. Mac was negotiating with Dan Haughton, CEO of Lockheed, for the purchase of a Jetstar for the company's Tiny Business Air Transport System. "Dan," he said, "how about selling us one for cost?" Haughton is said to have replied, "Mac, you couldn't afford it."

Recollections of
COURTLAND D. PERKINS

Retired Professor, Department Chairman, and
Associate Dean of Engineering, Princeton University:
Former Assistant Secretary of the Air Force
and Former President of the National Academy
of Engineering

The aeronautical and then the aerospace industry during the past 50 years has been led by an extraordinary group of powerful men. These included Donald Douglas, Glenn Martin, Dutch Kindleberger (North American Aviation), Bill Allen (Boeing), Jack Northrop and Robert Gross (Lockheed), Leroy Grumman, and Chance Vought (LTV). None of these were, in the long run, more successful or more extraordinary than James Smith McDonnell, who burst on the aeronautical scene in 1939 long after the others were firmly established, and he outperformed many of them. He died at the age of 81 on August 22, 1980, still chairman of his wonderful creation, the McDonnell Douglas Corporation, one of the largest aerospace companies in the nation.

It has always fascinated me to consider how he was able to wriggle his way into an already tightly held community involving defense and commercial air transportation companies and, in a short time, dominate some aspects of this field. In his early career, Jim McDonnell slowly accumulated a technical education, learned about flying by earning his wings with the Army Air Service, discovered how to design and build airplanes—first on his own and then through various project jobs that culminated in his position of Chief Project Engineer for Land Planes of the Glenn L. Martin Company of Baltimore.

He had gone to Princeton University and received a B.S. degree with honors in physics in 1921 and, after receiving his wings as a reserve second lieutenant in 1924, went to M.I.T. as a graduate student, receiving his M.S. in aeronautical engineering in 1925. His many sporadic flying jobs, his design work with several airplane companies, culminating in his experience at Martin, gave him the broad background necessary to embark on his own. This he did in 1939, forming the McDonnell Aircraft Corporation in St. Louis.

He started out with no programs but with a burning ambition to design and build airplanes. He took with him from the Martin Company several very able young engineers—Rene Miller, Abe Hyatt, Ivan Driggs, and others. He soon added more young engineers of great competence, including Kendall Perkins (no relation), George Graff, and David Lewis. One of his great capabilities was identifying and hiring the very best young engineers, and they joined "the team" as he called them. They and almost everyone else soon referred to him with affection as "Mr. Mac."

Mr. Mac was a man of sound technical capability, was meticulous in following the work of his engineers, was able to maintain tight fiscal control of his fledgling company, and had the courage to start fighting his way into a major role in this field. He was a good salesman, had good instincts as to what he should do and how to do it. He picked St. Louis for his operations, partially because he understood that large plants on our coasts might be considered vulnerable, and from the start was anxious to develop an image of being both an Army Air Forces and a Navy contractor with a foot in both camps.

One of his first projects was to develop a proposal for the Army Air Forces for a large fighter on which he was subsequently turned down. In the meantime, he kept his small plant and team operational by taking on subcontracts for airplane components from Douglas and Boeing and had many of his young engineers involved on front line research in various areas of aeronautical technology. While earning his wings with the Army Air Service, he met and made friends with many officers who had become factors on the development scene at Wright Field.

His persistence and clever choice of projects finally resulted in a contract by the Army Air Forces to develop a large fighter somewhat along the lines of his original proposal. This was his first major airplane program and it became the XP-67, a twin-engine, large fighter he called the "Bomber Destroyer." It had two Continental XI-1430 engines with superchargers developing some 1,600 horsepower. It is interesting to speculate on why the Army Air Forces at Wright Field gave such a contract to this fledgling company with no experience in building anything except components under subcontract. Without doubt, it was due to the approach of World War II, which made such contracts possible, but it also dealt with the many

friends Mr. Mac had made with Army Air Forces officers
and a growing feeling at Wright Field that this new company was worth taking a chance with. The XP-67 had difficult development pains, particularly with the engines,
which tended to catch on fire with alarming regularity.
The airplane became famous for its generous contouring
of the wing into the nacelles and the fuselage. It was called
by many "The Flying Fillet."

Now occurred one of the technical breakthroughs that
changed the whole field of airplane design and operations.
But more importantly, it was the event that changed the
whole character of the McDonnell Aircraft Corporation.
This was the advent of the gas turbine in 1939-1940. A
model of this British invention by Sir Frank Whittle was
brought to this country and given to General Electric in
Lynn, Massachusetts, where they developed a new version of this engine that was called the I-A. This engine
was given over to Bell Aircraft and their innovative designer, Larry Bell. He built an airplane around this engine
which became the P-59, our first pure jet airplane. The
P-59 made its first flight in October 1942. The Army Air
Forces asked Bell to do this probably because of its innovative climate and the fact that the other contractors were
heavily involved with building up production and would
not have responded so quickly to the new concept.

The same thing happened in the Navy. It had now heard
of the new gas turbine but was somewhat skeptical of its
value. Again, it didn't want to disturb its major contractors who had difficult production problems confronting

them. The Navy, probably influenced by Ivan Driggs who had left McDonnell Aircraft Corporation as chief engineer to head up the preliminary design office in the Bureau of Aeronautics, called in Mr. Mac. The Navy probably felt that this new, small, innovative company might be just the group to work on this new concept of a jet-propelled fighter that could operate off an aircraft carrier. The navy contacted Mr. Mac in early 1943 and had them send a design team in to the Navy Department to develop a proposal. This team, under Kendall Perkins, did come up with a workable design which was bought by the Navy and became the XFD-1 Phantom. This airplane first flew in January 1945 and later demonstrated that it could indeed operate off a carrier. The Navy was so pleased that it gave McDonnell Aircraft a contract to build 60 FD-1 (later FH-1) production models. This was the event that really got the company into the big league. As it was ready, it continued its growth to the present time. They built the Phantom, the Banshee, and then the Demon; later this led to their super success, the F-4 class, or Phantoms. The F-4 was in a desperate competition race with the Chance Vought F8U-3. This competition turned largely on the question of two engines and two place, versus one engine and single place. The two place won out and led to billions of dollars worth of business for McDonnell Aircraft augmented by an even larger buy from the U.S. Air Force.

But what about the Air Force? The XP-67 was really a failure but did get a McDonnell toe in the development door at Wright Field. Near the end of World War II, the

Army Air Forces gave McDonnell a contract to develop a large jet fighter designed for bomber escort. This design became the XF-88 and was in development at the end of World War II. Its progress was slowed, but it finally flew in October 1948. This airplane was developed slowly and when the J-57 engines became available, emerged as the F-101 or Voodoo. This was a very successful airplane and solidified McDonnell's position with the Air Force. The company had now grown from almost nothing in 1939 to one of the major aircraft suppliers to the Air Force and the Navy, and it has maintained this position.

Its great start was due to many factors that included the many competencies of Mr. Mac—his courage and determination to succeed, his ability to attract bright young associates and, finally, considerable luck. He was the unquestioned leader in this great success story and it continued to grow. He was selected to build our first manned space vehicles, Mercury and Gemini, and did a lot of development on missile re-entry vehicles. All of this culminated in his taking over the famous Douglas Aircraft Company that, through a complicated series of financial disasters, had become almost bankrupt. This merger resulted in the formation of the McDonnell Douglas Corporation, then one of the biggest aerospace companies in the country. The headquarters was kept in St. Louis, and Mr. Mac was the chairman of the board and chief executive officer.

My first personal contact with Mr. Mac was during World War II at Wright Field in connection with the

McDonnell entry to an Army Air Corps competition, the XP-88. Mr. Mac came to the Aircraft Laboratory to discuss his airplane with Bob Hage, then head of the Aircraft Performance Section, and myself, then head of the Stability and Control Section. We also included Major John Aldridge, project officer on the XP-88 and a good friend of Hage's and mine. The XP-88 never made it, but Mr. Mac set about hiring John Aldridge, Bob Hage, and me for when the war was over. Aldridge accepted, Bob Hage joined up some years later, and I resisted as I was set on joining the Princeton faculty. Over the next years, Mr. Mac tried to hire me on several occasions, either to join his "team" directly or to help run his Technical Advisory Board. I was never able to accept any of these offers. One day after I turned down his latest offer, he asked me how much it would take to get me to work for him. With tongue in cheek, I suggested about $250,000 a year. He said that I apparently didn't want to work for him at all. I said that I really didn't as I enjoyed my life at Princeton University and my ancillary activities. Mr. Mac was a good friend, and we enjoyed each other very much. He helped me in many ways with the Aeronautical Engineering Department at Princeton and, later, with the growth of the National Academy of Engineering—but I didn't want to work for him!

Another of my favorite anecdotes about Mr. Mac deals with a visit I made to McDonnell Aircraft while I was Assistant Secretary of the Air Force, R & D. I was in California and about to return to Washington, D.C. As the

Air Force airplane, a Convair 440, had to make a stop en route, I called my good friend, Bob Hage, then a vice president of McDonnell, saying that I would land at St. Louis and use the McDonnell flight facility for refueling. If convenient, I would spend the night with Bob and his lovely wife, Ginna. It was convenient, so I flew on into St. Louis. I was met by a big black Cadillac, a chauffeur and a young P.R. man. On leaving the SAM aircraft, I said to the P.R. man that Mr. Mac was getting more liberal with his officers—giving them the use of the company Cadillac. He then told me that this was Mr. Mac's Cadillac, and I was to spend the night with Mr. Mac and not with Bob and Ginna Hage. He said Mr. Mac had called Hage to "suggest" this new arrangement and that Bob had agreed. I then said that this new arrangement was not all right with me and that if I couldn't stay with my friends, the Hages, I would get back in the airplane and return to Washington. The young P.R. man seemed shaken by this and said, "Well, if you do that, take me with you!" I spent the night with the McDonnells.

These anecdotes are given to try to show his domination over his "team." Some of his top staff couldn't take this sort of thing, but most of them could and they were loyal to him and he to them when they needed it. He was an extraordinary, complex man who achieved much before he died in 1980. His legacy is the powerful McDonnell Douglas Corporation and the many national institutions that he supported over the years. A truly great man who made many contributions to the nation over the years.